The Underrepresentation of Women in Leadership Positions

Dr. LaShanda N. Shaw

Penning Grace Publishing

The Underrepresentation of Women in Leadership Positions
Copyright ©2022 by Dr. LaShanda N. Shaw

Published by Penning Grace Publishing, LLC
Fayetteville, NC 28306
www.penninghisgrace.com

Cover designed by MRF Graphics

All rights reserved. This book or parts thereof may not be reproduced in any form, stored in any retrieval system, or transmitted in any form by any means—electronic, mechanical, photocopy, recording, or otherwise—without prior written permission of the author.

Contact the Author for permission at LaShanda.Shaw@yahoo.com
www.lashandashaw.wixsite.com/drlashandashaw

Dr. LaShanda N. Shaw
ISBN Paperback 979-8-9851262-8-0
ISBN eBook 979-8-9851262-9-7

Library of Congress Control Number: 2022914901

The Underrepresentation of Women in Leadership Positions/
Dr. LaShanda N. Shaw

Dedication

I would like to dedicate this book to my family & especially my mom Cynthia Denise Shaw who always stuck by my side. To the many Professors that I have had upon this journey who assisted me in my Doctoral Education. And finally, I would like to thank Ms. Metoya Scott and Merlene May who have become true and dear friends to me over a short period of time, who assisted me in finding my interviewees and for that I will always be grateful to you.

Acknowledgements

I would like to first acknowledge God because I would be nowhere without him. To my Committee Members Dr. Les Huffman, Dr. Shawn Boone, and Dr. Marcia Hill, I would like to say thank you for assisting me along my dissertation journey, and for your patience with me. Lastly, I would like to thank the ten dynamic women that gave me the opportunity to interview them.

Table of Contents

Dedication 3

Acknowledgements 4

The Leaky & Blocked Corporate Pipeline 9

Theories that Keep Women Bound 14

History Says Men Can Only Be Leaders 18

Mentorship 28

Executive Leadership 30

Advertising Leadership 34

Educational Leadership 36

Entrepreneurship Leadership 41

Healthcare Leadership 43

Hospitality Leadership 46

National Government Leadership 48

Science Leadership 51

Sports Leadership 53

Women in Leadership: Their Story 55

Women Overcame Challenges Through Family Support 76

Women Overcoming Barriers Due to their Characteristics 78

Recommendations to Leaders and Practitioners .. 80

Recommendations for Future Research 83

References 86

Definition of Terms 120

About the Author 122

Connect with the Author 124

Introduction

The purpose of this book is to examine the challenges and barriers women who obtained leadership positions faced during their career journey, and how they overcame the challenges. While researching this topic, I examined the experiences and perceptions of women who were in senior- level positions from different industries.

The goal of the study was to find out what challenges or barriers these women who obtained leadership positions faced during their career journey and how these women overcame the challenges or barriers to attain their leadership positions.

Gaining new knowledge about women's experiences with gender bias, role stereotypes and any other obstacles may assist current and future generations of women that aspire to obtain leadership positions. The focus of the study had been to explore the individual experiences of women who held leadership positions. The topic is important to me because being a woman, I have experienced some of the pitfalls, bias, and gender discrimination in the workplace, as I strived to obtain a leadership position. It is the utmost importance and my duty to bring the subject more to the forefront. This subject has been talked and written about for years but there has not been any real resolution to the problem. Through my studies, I hope to start more dialogue with others, organizations, etc. to start a real change with this problem.

~Dr. LaShanda N. Shaw

Chapter 1

The Leaky & Blocked Corporate Pipeline

After years of advocacy, women continue to fight for equal rights and the ability to work the same jobs as their male counterparts (AAUW, 2016). However, leadership opportunities for women in America have been far less numerous than that of men, this has been attributed to gender discrimination (Wolfe, 2019). Gender discrimination at work occurs whenever an individual is treated differently on account of their gender and may affect anything from hiring decisions to promotions (Wolfe, 2019).

Gender discrimination was the most significant reason women are not represented in more leadership positions (Ibarra, Carter, & Silva, 2010). Workplace gender discrimination has continued to be a major problem, even though there have been laws passed, such as Title VII or the Equal Pay Act forbidding workplace gender discrimination (Wolfe, 2019). Under U.S. law, Title VIII of the Civil Rights Act of 1964 had prohibited the discrimination of any employee based on gender (Wolfe, 2019).

According to a survey completed by TNS Research 68% of the women surveyed believed gender discrimination existed in the workplace, some of the effects of gender discrimination are a loss of motivation and morale necessary to perform the job effectively (Gluck, 2014).

Jodi L. Jacobson of the World Watch Institute revealed in a written report that gender bias led to a loss of productivity (Gluck, 2014). Despite women's success in middle management, most have not been able to be promoted to senior-level leadership positions within organizations which include CEOs and Board Members (Shellenbarger, 2018). Virginia Schein, Professor of Management at Gettysburg College in Gettysburg, Pennsylvania, believed gender stereotyping created most of the managerial barriers for females (Schein, 2015).

<u>Malhotra (2017), a chairman at McKinsey and Co., has said, "For women, the corporate talent pipeline was leaky and blocked (Malhotra, 2017 as cited by Zenger, 2019, p.1).</u>

Leadership positions had been a predominately masculine role of where few females have been able to earn (Eagly & Karau, 2002). A few women such as Irene Rosenfeld, Chairman and CEO of Kraft Foods, and Indra Nooyi, Chairman and CEO of PepsiCo had stood out in their performance within a business world that was dominated by male leaders (Schein, 2015).

These women were able to breakdown barriers and helped to advance females in leadership positions. As the landscape of corporate America continues to change, a lack of female board members could limit an organization's external resources due to not being gender diverse

(Catalyst, 2019). Based on the January 2019 S&P list, women held 24 (4.8%) of CEO positions (Catalyst, 2019). Due to family obligations, women may not have been able to join the same social networks as men, which can lead to promotions in many cases, since these interactions routinely take place after hours (Catalyst, 2019).

The problem is the underrepresentation of women in executive leadership positions, resulting in that number of women who hold seats on boards or in senior management positions, are decreasing (Catalyst, 2019). Understanding the perceptions of women who made it to an executive leadership position, could lead to an increase in gender diversity within executive leadership positions, by informing promotion practices to help ensure fairness.

Executive Leadership

Executive leadership is something that few have been able to accomplish but especially for women. Researchers inside and outside of academics agreed to leadership positions as it is narrow and full of twists and turns and included negative gender stereotypes to cultural barriers (Eagly & Carli, 2007). Women are communal, which is gentle, affectionate, and soft spoken, which are characteristics not deemed as appropriate for effective leadership (Haines, Deaux, & Lofaro, 2016).

Men characteristics ranging from self-confident and aggressive, which are more associated with leadership (Haines, Deaux, & Lofaro, 2016).
For the first time in history, women represented half of all United States workers (Kiene, 2016). Mothers were the primary earners or co-earners in nearly two-thirds of

American families (Kiene, 2016). Women were equal or the main earner in nearly four out of ten families with children (National Partnership, 2017).

Women had attained higher education levels than men, yet they made a considerably less salary than men (Ward, 2019). The median annual income for a woman who held a full-time job was $36,113 while the median income for a man who held a full-time job was $42,039 (National Partnership, 2017). The results showed that women were paid 86 cents for every dollar paid to men, for which had come to an annual wage gap of $5,926 (National Partnership, 2017). Research typically listed the population of women in leadership positions by countries or regions but did not by state and county (National Partnership, 2017). The results of the researcher's study aim were to explore the reasons why women are underrepresented in leadership positions and for companies to be made aware of the benefits of gender diversity among their leaders.

The significance of the study of leadership was to bridge the gap between women and men in leadership positions. Leadership is something that should have been fairly attained by both males and females alike (Kim & Starks, 2016). Different perspectives and different backgrounds may had helped to achieve a more diverse and successful organization (Kim & Starks, 2016).

Differences between men and women maybe attributed to evolutionary stressors that contributed to the development of relationships and task-oriented tendencies (Forsyth, 2014). Eagly and Carli (2007) found that these differences caused gender bias and discrimination against women which led to less pay and fewer opportunities for promotion.

The standards have been easier for men as evidenced by them attaining leadership positions in greater numbers leading to top executive jobs (Forsyth, 2014). This is despite a higher average of exceptionally skilled women who have been passed over and discriminated against (Forsyth, 2014).

Chapter 2

Theories That Keep Women Bound

Four theories covered various ideas of what happens to women in leadership or why women are not in leadership. These theories were developed overtime from the experience in the workplace, in addition to the perceptions of what kept women bound in the workplace. The following theories will be further defined and addressed.

Glass Ceiling Theory

Hull and Umansky wrote the influential study in regard to glass ceiling theory in 1997. The glass ceiling referred to the set of social and organizational pressures that formed barriers that excluded women from upper-level management positions in organizations (Hull & Umansky, 1997). The Glass Ceiling Theory, in the amendment of the "Civil Rights Act of 1991" the Federal Glass Ceiling Commission (FGCC) was born, the responsibility of the commission was to identify barriers of the glass ceiling (FGCC, 1995, p. 5).

The Commission defined the glass ceiling as an

invisible barrier that prevented women from being promoted to executive level positions even if they were qualified to do so (FGCC, 1995). A report showed that the Glass Ceiling affected two thirds of the female population (FGCC, 1995).

The Glass Cliff Theory
The glass cliff theory written by Smith in 2015, stemmed from research on private sector organizations which could have been used to understand the circumstances in private organizations (Smith, 2015). The Glass Cliff theory suggested that when women did get into leadership positions, it was usually an organization that had gone through a crisis and where the risk of failure was also higher (Smith, 2015). The national sample of local education agencies study, found evidence and support for the Glass Cliff Theory (Smith, 2015).

The Glass Escalator Theory
Blackburn wrote the important work on glass escalator theory in 2017. The glass escalator theory referred to how men in female-dominated careers, such as teaching and nursing, often rose higher and faster than women in male-dominated fields (Blackburn, 2017). There were various explanations for this phenomenon which included those women who had more "career interruptions," such as leaving work to care for their children (Blackburn, 2017).

Another explanation that was given for the glass escalator theory by Caren Goldberg, who was an assistant professor of management, is that "stereotypes about what prototypical man was matched with stereotypes about what a prototypical manager was (Blackburn, 2017 p. 1)." The notion was that in a female-dominated career field, there were few people who fit those stereotypes but males, which had caused males to be noticed more and promoted quicker up the leadership chain (Blackburn, 2017).

Role Congruity Theory

The role congruity theory considered the gender role of the individual, its congruity with other roles, and behavior that was prejudicially associated with the role. Eagly and Karau (2002), who wrote the seminal work on this theory in 2002, found that women who were leaders was perceived in a less positive manner when compared to male leaders.

Eagly and Karau (2002) showed that women had a more difficult time achieving high-status positions in the workplace.

Sex-Role Stereotypes Theory

Naffziger and Naffziger wrote the seminal work on sex-role stereotypes in 1974.. Research on sex-role stereotypes revealed men were more competent while women were more sex-role stereotypes warm or expressive (Naffziger & Naffziger, 1974; Scantlebury, 2009). At that time, masculinity and femininity were opposites. Men were expected to be masculine; women were expected to be feminine, and anyone who fell in the middle was considered maladjusted or in need of help (Naffziger & Naffziger, 1974; Scantlebury, 2009).

The various theories discussed provide the background for why women are still underrepresented in leadership positions. The themes discussed include the barriers and challenges that women faced. The barriers and challenges included being put in organizations where the company was already failing. Women being able to make it to certain a level in organizations but can't move any further due to women not being seen as leaders.

Ibarra, Carter, and Silva (2010) viewed gender discrimination was the most prominent reason women were not present in more leadership positions. Even though women had succeeded in positions in middle management, most had not been able to move beyond that level (Gluck, 2014).

Chapter 3

History Says Men Can Only Be Leaders

Leadership has roots at the beginning of civilization. Early philosophical writings from Plato's Republic to Plutarch's Lives have explored the question "What qualities distinguish an individual as a leader?" (Carlyle & Galton, 1841, p.14).

At this same time, the idea that leadership is based on certain characteristics is known as the trait theory of leadership (Carlyle & Galton, 1841). The trait theory was explored in the 19th century in various works, most notably by Thomas Carlyle and Francis Galton. Carlyle identified the talents, skills, and physical characteristics of men who rose to power.

Galton (1869) examined leadership qualities in the families of powerful men, after showing the numbers of eminent relatives declined when moving from first degree to second-degree relatives, Galton concluded leadership was inherited. Leaders were born, not developed (Galton, 1869).

Both notable works offered great support for the notion that leadership is rooted in the characteristics of the leader. This early theory not only validated the idea that leaders were born to be leaders, but also leaders could only be men (Galton, 1869).

Manufacturing Leadership

Women in the manufacturing industry were of importance to this research because this is where most women got their start at working (McComb-DiPesa, 2005). Between 1930 and 1945, women workers' experiences in the labor force and organized labor were shaped. During World War II, women were working in the manufacturing industry due to men being absent at war (McComb-DiPesa, 2005).

In the Depression era, manufacturing industries recovered much faster than heavier industries like steel and rubber, which were dominated by men, which meant women loss less jobs than men at this time (McComb-DiPesa, 2005). During this era, more women were pushed to go to work being that their husbands were laid off or received extreme pay cuts (McComb- DiPesa, 2005).

By the 1940s; due to the New Deal's Congress of Industrial Organizations (CIO) assisting women and men in getting unionized in auto, glass, leather, rubber industries, 800,000 American women were unionized (McComb-DiPesa, 2005). While the New Deal improved women's experiences in the industry, they were still plagued with sexism and racism, and therefore prejudices against women were preserved (McComb-DiPesa, 2005). Women's wages were raised more than they were before the Depression, but it was still not equal to men's wages (McComb-DiPesa, 2005).

During the 1950s, women held steady in the manufacturing industry, they felt a sense of pride enjoyed the confidence and freedom of working for a living. They fought hard to keep their factory work, even though they were still getting paid a lot less than their male counterpart (McComb-DiPesa, 2005). During this time, women assisted in production, such as the construction of cars and appliances (McComb-DiPesa, 2005). By the 1970s women began to flood colleges and grad schools (McComb-DiPesa, 2005). They began to enter professions such as medicine, law, dental, and business that were once dominated by males. At this point, women saw these careers as professions and started to leave manufacturing (McComb-DiPesa, 2005).

The manufacturing industry is one that has always held the perception of being male dominated; this is one of the reasons that is cited in a study by Deloitte and the Manufacturing Institute that is the key driver of women's underrepresentation in this industry (Christnacht & Laughlin, 2017). In a study conducted by Bayer in 2012 other factors noted as to why there is an underrepresentation of women in the manufacturing industry found that some women shun manufacturing careers due to the lack of quality of science and math education programs, and due to the lingering, outdated stereotypes regarding manufacturing careers as unsuitable for women (Christnacht & Laughlin, 2017). These stereotypes persisted even though according to Cleveland Plain Dealer, that girls perform better in math and science than boys do in the lower grades (Schelmetic, 2012).

Women made up nearly one-third of the

manufacturing industry workforce (Christnacht & Laughlin, 2017). Although women make up almost half of the working population, they are still underrepresented in the manufacturing industry (Christnacht & Laughlin, 2017). In 2014, Mara Barra became the first CEO of General Motors in the United States and the first woman to run a major auto maker (Christnacht & Laughlin, 2017).

Compared to a Catalyst Research survey of women in U.S. Manufacturing, which they have manufacturing defined as durable goods. Compared to women in U.S. business, women in the manufacturing sector were lagging in senior leadership positions compared to an already underrepresented sector of women in U.S. business altogether (Chapman, 2018). Only 24% of manufacturing companies have 40% or more female directors on the board, whilst 32% have female board representation of 25% or lower (Chapman, 2018).

Early philosophers found females inferior to males, but, by the 1960s, the feminist movement countered these findings. Men being stronger because their physical bodies are larger than women's (Eagly & Carli, 2007). Few females hold senior-level roles because they lack the aggressive characteristics needed to hold higher- level positions (Eagly & Carli, 2007).

Schein suggested gender stereotyping created many managerial barriers for females. Women made small strides in the 1970s and the 1980s by reaching middle management positions, but research suggested women are still often seen as fewer effective leaders, and men are viewed as better suited for decision-making tasks (Ibarra & Obodaru, 2009).

Women's representation has changed due to the changing role in the workplace. However, the subliminal message of a patriarchal ideology that continues to objectify women remains the same (Klenke, 2011). Women have made strides in the 21st century in leadership careers for women, yet leadership has still been an arduous journey (Klenke, 2011). Explanations for this included the Schain's (1973) "Think Manager – Think Male Paradigms."

In another study done women were less likely to be successful as managers than men. This study had focused on a lack of qualified women as a contributing factor to the gender gap. Showing that women do not have enough education and work experience to be selected.

Grooming in School

Grooming for leadership roles starts early (Baker, 2013). Evidence of men being groomed for leadership can be found early on in the educational system (Baker, 2013). Boys are more likely to be groomed in school as leaders (Baker, 2013). This grooming began with teacher-student interactions, which show the clearest form of classroom inequities (Baker, 2013). In studies done by Dale Baker a fellow of American Association for the Advancement of Science and the American Educational Research Association in classrooms show that teachers call on boys more frequently than they do girls and ask boys higher-order questions (Baker, 2013).

Boys receive more extensive feedback, and teachers use longer wait-time with boys than girls. Teachers limit the interactions of girls to more non-academic and social topics (Baker, 2013). Girls rarely are chosen to give a demonstration or help with an experiment while boys receive more teacher attention than girls (Baker, 2013).

This behavior increases as students move from elementary to junior and senior high school. Even non-verbal teacher behaviors, such as head nodding and encouraging smiles, favor boys over girls. These actions relate to the low self-esteem of girls and the higher self-esteem of boys, which will aid them in becoming leaders (Baker, 2013).

Gender Social Status

The author recognized theories about gendered social status that has more of barring of the underrepresentation of female leaders. Women were lower status than men, the status is important because this influences how individuals perceive one another which can have a direct bearing on the competencies in society (Powell, 2014).

According to Ely (1995), power and status differentials between men and women will continue as long as the underrepresentation of women in leadership positions persists in organizations, due to these males are going to have more of a say so on who gets promoted. Theories contributed to this include social identity which says that once individuals form their social group, they conduct similar social behaviors (Vinney, 2018). Threat rigidity theory which states that individuals within groups tend to behave rigidly when they are faced with a threat (Vinney, 2018).

The Queen Bee Syndrome is a negative

relationship among women in senior management positions and their female subordinates (Gaeun & Seung-Hyun, 2017).

Women have shown to have a lower Affective Motivation to Lead (a-Mil) which is shown to have a direct correlation to leadership (Elprana et al., 2015). The theory was introduced by Chan and Drasgrow in 2001, which is the specific motivation to assume leadership responsibilities (Chan & Drasgrow, 2001). Affective Motivation to Lead is predicted by personality, sociocultural values, leadership experience, and self-efficacy (Chan & Drasgrow, 2001).

In a study done at a high school and university, students show that highly traditional beliefs about gender roles were related with a lower a- M+L. Social Potency is the most identified personality trait when it comes to leadership (Baker, 2015). Social Potency is defined as social dominance or interpersonal power and a desire to make an impact on others (Baker, 2015). People who have social potency have strong personality traits and are described as decisive, forceful and able to influence others (Baker, 2015). In a study of 124 completed surveys done by female students which was measured using the multidimensional personality questionnaire, social potency was shown to have a direct effect on leadership self-efficacy (Baker, 2015).

Women in the study who had more leadership confidence was more likely to ascribe themselves to someone who is socially dominate and someone who can engage with others (Baker, 2015). The notion of this study was that if young women could see where they stood regarding their social potency through a tailored assessment like the one that was done in this study that they could be well informed in their educational and career planning (Baker, 2015).

Organizational Culture has been a barrier for women in the workplace and those aspiring for leadership positions (Servere et al., 2016). Sexual harassment has intimidated
women aspiring to leadership positions in organizations (Servere et al., 2016). Other factors include organizations not capitalizing on the talents of women in the workforce (Servere et al., 2016). General norms and cultural barriers were another barrier such as cultural practices, religious prohibitions, social stratification, and ethnic prejudice (Servere et al., 2016).

Often women who were talented are put in human resource management instead of more senior-level positions (Servere et al., 2016). Some countries are making strides to promote women to senior-level positions such as China. In fact, 76% of women in China aspire to top-level leadership position compared to only 52% of the United States (Servere et al., 2016).

Transformational Leadership Theory

The theory of transformational leadership was introduced by James Burns in 1978 (Cherry, 2018). Transformational leadership may be defined as a leadership approach that causes a change in individuals and social systems (Burns, 1978 as cited by Cherry, 2018). This style is said to create valuable and positive change in "followers" with a potential result that these followers become the leaders. This theory was extremely popular with female leaders. In early studies, from the late 1980s and early 1990s, it was found that women adopted participative styles of leadership and were more transformational leaders than men who adopted more directive and transactional styles of leadership (Cherry, 2018).

Women in management positions tended to place more emphasis on communication, cooperation, affiliation, and nurturing than men as well as having more communal qualities (Badura et al., 2018). Transformational leadership roles are what women in leadership position leadership style usually lends to.

Initially, women were not seen as leaders (Carlyle & Galton, 1841). Men were considered natural leaders and assumed almost every leadership position in society (Carlyle & Galton, 1841). In schools that are coeducational, boys are more likely to be picked to answer questions and get more attention than girls (Baker, 2013). Women have been underrepresented in leadership positions even though they hold a greater number of advanced degrees. The lack of women in leadership is attributed to the lack of mentorship, women not being leaders, the Queen Bee Syndrome, and Gender Bias (Thornton, 2016).

The history of the underrepresentation of women in leadership positions has been identified as far back as the early 1800s. Leadership has been a predominately masculine role through centuries that few females have reached (Eagly & Karau, 2002). Included in this chapter were leadership models such as transformational leadership theory which was introduced by James Burns in 1978 (Cherry, 2018).

Transformational leadership may be defined as a

leadership approach that causes a change in individuals and social systems. This theory is immensely popular with female leaders. In early studies, from the late 1980s and early 1990s, it was found that women adopted participative styles of leadership and were more transformational leaders than men who adopted more directive and transactional styles of leadership (Cherry, 2018).

Chapter 4

Mentorship

There are over 165,000 articles on leadership but only 5% that address leadership and gender-related issues (Thornton, 2016). Worldwide women held less than a quarter of senior leadership positions and a third are not women at all in senior roles (Grant Thornton, 2016). Past literature has focused on stereotyping, gender bias, and discrimination as reasons for a gender gap amongst women.

Another research has shown that there maybe a pipeline problem (Thornton, 2016). Women have been receiving more degrees than men since 2000, 57% of bachelor's degrees, 59.9% of all master's degrees and 51.8% of all doctorate degrees (National Center for Education Statistics, 2016). Even though this being the case women are underrepresented when it comes to MBAs with women only making up a third of MBA degrees (Gipson et al., 2017).

Women have the education but lack in the experience compared to males (Gipson et al., 2017). Women made up half of middle managers but get stuck there, which could have to do with corporate policies and practices, or unconscious biases and stereotypes (Gipson et al., 2017). When women were selected for these leadership positions, they are usually in a support function and less visible (Gipson et al., 2017).

Lack of publications on how to develop women leaders, but the publications tend to focus on recommendations that organizations should create and implement instead of implementing and evaluating said recommendations (Gipson et al., 2017). The Multi rater feedback, executive coaching, mentorship and networking can assist women in leadership development (Gipson et al., 2017).

Multi rater feedback is used to enhance self-awareness by gathering feedback from superiors, peers, and others in the organization, this is a chance for women to gain honest feedback (Gipson et al., 2017). An executive coach assists in designing a development plan that leverages the individual's strengths and corrects any identified weaknesses (Gipson et al., 2017).

Mentorship is a relationship between two people in which the mentor is usually experienced and can provide "technical & psychological support (Gipson et al., 2017)." Networking is important in leadership and leadership development because membership in certain networks often provide opportunities to build relationships (Gipson et al., 2017).

Chapter 5

Executive Leadership

Women have seen an improvement between 1970 to 2012, in their total employment from 37% to 47% (Gaeun & Seung-Hyun, 2017). In 2012 there were 51.4% of women working in management positions but they are still underrepresented at executive and board positions (Metz, et al. 2014).

Women occupy only 14.6% of executive officer positions of Fortune 500 Companies (Catalyst, 2016). Out of the 500 companies only 23 companies are led by female CEOs (Catalyst, 2016a). In studies conducted it shows that having more women in these executive positions produces a positive impact on business growth (Catalyst, 2016). In addition, women in executive positions provided role models for high-potential women. Some studies try to show that gender differences in leadership styles contribute to the underrepresentation (Catalyst, 2016). But in recent years studies showed that there are more similarities than differences in the leadership styles of men and women (Oshagbem et al., 2014).

Women and minorities have been underrepresented in a facet of areas of corporate leadership however by some metrics, there has been some recent progress of women and minorities represented on corporate boards (Cohen, 2018). Women and minorities, however, were still underrepresented in the most elite and powerful board seats, including board chair and chair (Cohen, 2018). Women were still also underrepresented in the C- Level positions including the CEO (Cohen, 2018). Also, although women and minorities may now have one board seat, they still are underrepresented in having those who hold more than one corporate board seat (Akutagawa, et. al, 2019).

Individuals who had one board seat compared to ones who have multiple ones are quite different, as to have multiple board seats puts them in the corporate elite or the in-crowd as seen by corporate leaders. Which in returned these corporate elite will have the influence over corporate policies, etc.

Women and minorities represent 28% and 22% of those who hold one board seat and 8 and 5% of those who hold multiple board seats (Cohen, 2018). Women who were first-time Directors are seen to get significantly lower levels of mentoring than white males (Cohen, 2018). First time Directors were 72% less likely to get assistance of other Directors to get the CEOs "okay" before raising concerns or questions in formal meetings (McDonald & Westphal, 2013). In the ways to do this was by clearing concerns with the CEO before meetings and not just letting it be the first time it is being introduced and letting them give the okay (Cohen, 2018).

Ways that first-time Directors may have learn of this is through informal mentoring (Cohen, 2018). In the absence of an experienced mentor, first-time Directors would find it difficult to learn the corporate norms, which will lead to a negative first impression (Cohen, 2018). Since women got fewer mentoring opportunities, they will be at a disadvantage. White males that are first- time Directors are perceived as being in the in group because boards mimic their appearance, while women and minorities are seen in the out group (Cohen, 2018).

Over the years there has been a positive change of women residing on boards in other countries but the number of women who hold senior executive ranks are still low (Klettner et al., 2014). Do we simply want more women in leadership, or do we want to encourage cultural change within the business sector, is an on-going question that has been posed (Klettner et al., 2014). The authors of the article *Strategic and Regulatory Approaches to Increasing Women in Leadership* think that its best to have a more flexible and voluntary regime opposed to mandatory regulations which could be more effective (Klettner et al., 2014).

In Norway there had been a 40% quota that has been achieved, but in 2009 the percentage of women on boards had not increased which shows that quota hasn't had any real effect on the number of women in executive positions (Klettner et al., 2014). Since 2010, Australia had seen an increase in female board members (Klettner et al., 2014).

This had been accomplished through the development of programs for mentorship and networking, professional training and changes to the process of recruitment and leave processes, these things have been designed to counter the subtle discrimination that remains in business culture today and thereby improve equal opportunity (Klettner et al., 2014).

Chapter 6

Advertising Leadership

Women only made up 20% of advertising creative departments worldwide (Torras & Grow, 2015). In Peru, the numbers are less than that with women comprising only between 3% to 10.4% (Torras & Grow, 2015). The author examined what could be the cause of this by looking at relationships with colleagues and clients, work/life balance and the environment within creative departments.

Creative departments in Peru had been deemed machismo (Mensa, 2015). One of the limitations of the article was that there are few studies on women in Peru and their underrepresentation in advertising creative departments. Men make up 89.6% while women make up only 10.4% in advertising creative departments (Mensa, 2015). In a study done at the University of Lima 82% of women believed that discrimination still existed (Mensa, 2015).

Studies also showed that when women feel alienated their creativity could not grow (Mensa, 2015).

Eight women were surveyed, seven were single and one was married with one child. These women described themselves as creative while characterizing the males as humorous (Mensa, 2015). Gender bias was prevalent in the findings from client and colleague relationships, to work/life balance, to advancement opportunities (Mensa, 2015).

Women in Lebanon face many barriers to leadership positions. Lebanese organizations operate on a "Think Male, Think Manager" (Maryssa et al., 2015). Organizations in Lebanese also neglect working arrangements such as flex time and childcare support (Tlaiss, 2014). The study examined 129 participants at a Lebanese University. Lebanese women are emotional and submissive individuals while men are balanced and autonomous (Tlaiss, 2014). Studies show that women and men both perceive men as a better fit in executive positions; women were also more likely than men to believe in women (Schein, 2001).

In the study 82.2% believed that women are not treated the same as men and 29.5% believed that men were more competent than women while only 5.4% believed that women were more competent than men (Tlaiss, 2014). In this study women said that they were discriminated against by other women and preferred to work with males (Tlaiss, 2014). Thirty-one percent of respondents believe that family-work life to be the second barrier (Tlaiss, 2014).

Chapter 7

Educational Leadership

Women earned 57.3% of master's degrees, and 53% of doctoral degrees (Perry, 2018). With their higher education, women should be advancing; however, this is not the case. Women were underrepresented in senior administrative positions in universities (Perry, 2018). Women in higher education leadership made up less than one-third at colleges and universities (Perry, 2018).

For women who had succeeded in their pursuit of university leadership positions, Tolar (2012) noted that these women identified mentoring as essential to their success, this study also showed that the lack of mentorships can be a detriment. Mentors help women remove or learn how to remove obstacles to higher- education leadership (Perry, 2018). These women in higher-education leadership described mentors as counselors and sources of inspiration (Perry, 2018). Not having mentors made these women feel less successful because they did not have anyone to look up to or to show them what was right from wrong (Perry, 2018).

In schools and universities across the UK women were underrepresented in leadership roles (Tickle, 2017). Women accounted for 45% of academic staff but only account for 22% of professors, 35% of deputy and pro vice-chancellors (PVCs) and 20% of vice chancellors for the 2013 and 2014 academic year (ECU, 2015a). The study centered around English universities that are pre-1992 where the proportions of females in leadership was a lot lower at the PCVs and heads level which make up 24% and 11% (Shepherd, 2014).

In some of the most prestigious universities the vice chancellor and all the PVCs were men (Shepherd, 2015b). Which is even though women made up more than half of higher education students (56%) and staff (54%) (Shepherd, 2015 b). Across Europe in the 27 countries only 15.5% of all higher education institutions and 10% of universities that award PhDs was headed by a woman (European University Association, 2017)). Studies found that the more women executives an organization has the better they perform (Noland et. al, 2016).

Another study done of recent university governor's equality and diversity wasn't seen as a concern; with only 3% of governors identify the issue as a key institutional challenge and only 17% (compared to 42% of staff) believe that it is harder for women to succeed than men in organizations (LFHE, 2015; pg. 15).

Savigny (2014) calculates that at the current growth rate of 0.75% per annum it will take 100 years and over for women to achieve equal numbers in the UK. Even though women are fewer in numbers at the PVC level they were no less likely to aspire to these positions as men. From a recent leadership foundation survey of alumni from its Top Management Program which was designed for aspiring university leaders' women cited a lack of confidence as factor in their career progression (Manfredi, et al., 2014). Other research shows that some women view management roles as unappealing, and overly demanding or simply non-do-able (Shepherd, 2017).

Female educational leaders developed their leadership practice during challenges they may face (Mahmood, 2015). The researcher's study provided educators various home-grown leadership models that can be used towards running an organization effectively in administration. Seven women were followed in this study as they went through a year of leadership training at the Qurban and Surray Educational Trust in Lahore, Pakistan. The leadership training was aimed at promoting justice, equality, peace and sustainable development, to encourage, and delegate (Mahmood, 2015). The question has been posed time and time again are leaders made or grown? And can women from constrained backgrounds learn to lead and aspire (Mahmood, 2015)?

After a year of leadership training the women were asked to describe and define their leadership styles. The reason for this was to formulate a leadership module for training purposes. Through the year training of women sharing their experiences, training, and perspectives the Qurban Leadership Models were produced. This assisted in finding their strengths and putting them into fruition to inspire these women to give them purpose, prioritizing their values, managing energy, expanding their horizons, gaining the resilience to move ahead even when things get hard, and being able to identify who can help them grow (Mahmood, 2015). The leadership training had helped these women spread their wings. The women noted that after this leadership training that they now had a self-confidence that they did not have before (Mahmood, 2015).

Over the years it has been well documented the slow progression of women in academics compared to men in this field (Nguyen & Huong, 2013). Some of the limitations that come with this was that that there is little known research on female academics in developing countries such as Vietnam (Nguyen & Huong, 2013). This was is an exploratory study that was funded by Cambridge – Vietnam Women Leadership Program, their aim was to aspire and empower female's academics managers in Vietnamese higher education (Nguyen & Huong, 2013). The study was largely based on what women in higher education leadership including university leaders and female Deans, perceived to be the barriers in female academics (Nguyen & Huong, 2013).

Researchers who are both inside and outside of academics agree that for women who aspire to leadership positions that there is a path but that its very narrow and full of twist and turns (Eagly & Carli, 2007, p. 64). The reasons that were given include negative gender stereotypes to cultural barriers (Nguyen & Huong, 2013). Women were communal, which is gentle, affectionate, and soft spoken which are characteristics that are not deemed as appropriate for effective leadership (Nguyen & Huong, 2013). Men on the other hand characteristics ranged from self-confident, aggressive, which are more associated with leadership (Nguyen & Huong, 2013).

Researchers showed that the "Think Manager – Think Male" attitude is very much alive today especially among males (Balgiu, 2013).

This same phenomenon can be used in other sectors just like in academics, "Think Professor - Think Male" and "Think Vice Chancellor - Think Male" (Nguyen & Houng, 2013). These views limited women's access to academic leadership roles and creates unfair bias in their evaluations when they do happen to receive these roles (Nguyen & Houng, 2013). It has also become of a two- edge sword with how women lead going from if they are communal then they lack the qualities to be an effective leader but then when they show some characteristics of their male counterparts then they are they lack empathy (Nguyen & Huong, 2013).

In more traditional societies as Vietnam women were expected to take on more family responsibility than the male (Mestechkina, et. al., 2014). One of the things that was deemed important from this article was that family support was a big factor in impeding or facilitation of female academic career progress in Vietnam. Strong appropriate policies and measures must take place in Vietnam and across the world to lessen the time demands of women's domestic work and childcare so that women can put as much effort into their careers as their male counterparts (Nguyen & Huong, 2013).

Chapter 8

Entrepreneurship Leadership

The purpose of this study was to evaluate what impact does mini companies have on young women and men about perceive durability and perceived feasibility of self-employment (Vegard, 2016). In Europe, The Company Program (CP) was the largest mini company organization in secondary schools (Vegard, 2016). Overall women were underrepresented compared to men in entrepreneurship (Vegard, 2016).

Entrepreneurship Education has seen an increase in secondary schools and higher education institutions in Europe throughout the decades (Martinez et al., 2010; Eurydice, 2012). In Europe the goal of the mini-companies is to combine practical and theoretical learning and stimulate collaboration between the schools and working people which are expected to contribute to the fulfilment of a range of policy objectives such as barriers to female entrepreneurship which include lack of support from institutions, family, support, etc. (Vegard, 2016).

The study showed that women are less likely to take risk than men which may be one of the reasons there lies a lack of women in Entrepreneurship (Vegard, 2016). Another reason is that a study shows that some women do not want to be Entrepreneurs because it is seen as less desirable for a woman to be one compared to a man (Vegard, 2016).

Obstacles that women faced include less female entrepreneur role models to aspire to be, disadvantages related to pregnancy, and women's personal goals and work life differ from that of their male counterparts (Johansen, 2013). In 2012, only 26% of women was involved in early stages of Entrepreneurship activities (Vegard, 2016).

In a study where 1,160 participants responded to a survey, the analysis showed that regard to perceived desirability of self-employment 35% of males had a high desire to become entrepreneurs compared to 24% of females (Vegard, 2016). The goal for EE is not for females to create a business immediately but hopefully that the mini-companies will spark the fire that will boost the chance of them attempting to start a business (Vegard, 2016).

Chapter 9

Healthcare Leadership

Although women have long had an influential impact on healthcare, the top executive roles in healthcare have generally eluded women (McDonagh, 2012). Women are still seen as nurturers and not as strong and confident as men (McDonagh, 2012).

These are the reasons given for the lack of women in leadership positions in the healthcare industry (McDonagh, 2012). In the new age of changes in healthcare, women, known as transformational leaders, are needed in leadership positions (Bobrowski et al., 2014). Even though the healthcare workforce is predominantly female, women only account for 12% of hospital CEOs (Lemak, 2016).

Women had traditionally faced obstacles, such as inhospitable corporate cultures, lack of leadership development opportunities, and lack of confidence, but have made some strides in reaching leadership positions (Lemak, 2016). It had created many challenges because of a lack of direction for women who aim for leadership positions (Lemak, 2016). Trying to deal with barriers has left women thinking they have to fend for themselves on this pathway or opt to abandon their pursuit of executive-level leadership positions (Lemak, 2016).

Women have increased in numbers of those entering the field of psychology (American Psychological Association, 2017). This study dived into the achievement motivations, loader identity, career salience, and willingness to compromise a career for partner and children. Women made up 67% of psychologists and 75% of enrolled doctoral students enrolled in a graduate program (American Psychological Association, 2017).

This being said women were still underrepresented in leadership positions in this field only comprising in 2014, 39.3% of the editors of fellows in the APA journals and 32.3% of fellows in the APA were women (APA Center for Workforce Studies, 2014a). In 2013 women only made up 30% of all full professors (APA Center for Workforce Studies, 2014a). There had been separate sections of APA that is focused on women, which supports them in social justice and equality (APA Center for Workforce Studies, 2014a).

The Committee of Women in Psychology was also introduced in 1973, to improve the status of women in Psychology (APA Center for Workforce Studies, 2014a). Despite these initiatives' women are still underrepresented. Reasons for this included discrimination, societal expectations, and institutional barriers (APA Center for Workforce Studies, 2014a). For some women they decided at a younger age to pursue less prestigious careers in exchange for a future family life. Women were also more likely than men to follow their partners for a job opportunity (Gregor & O'Brien, 2015). The study showed that there was a negative correlation emerged between general leadership aspirations and willingness to prioritize the needs of their partner when making career decisions (Gregor & O'Brien, 2015).

There were also differences between women who were in the early years of graduate program versus later doctoral study. In the later years, women were more likely to compromise their careers for their partner and family which could possibly be due to stress after completing the program (Gregor & O' Brien, 2015).

Chapter 10

Hospitality Leadership

The hospitality industry was the third largest employer in the United States (Gaille, 2017). In the United States alone nearly seven million people were employed in this industry (Gaille, 2017). Although the numbers were astounding women are still underrepresented in this industry in higher management positions (Gaille, 2017).

One reason was deemed that the Hospitality industry has long hours and frequent geographical moves, and it is difficult for women to take care of a family with kinds of demands (Gaille, 2017). Most of the ones in this industry who get to the top were single or divorced (Gaille, 2017). There are also indications that women had issues with masculine and feminine attributes stereotypes (Kachel et al., 2016). One woman said that you had to learn to be "tough" in this male dominated industry (Gaille, 2017).

Another issue was the supply barrier due to the lack of qualified women and minorities because of inequities in the nation's educational system (Gaille, 2017). According to the U.S Federal Glass Ceiling Commission, the third barrier is government barriers (Gaille, 2017). Even though in 1964, the Civil Rights Act outlined sexual discrimination in the U.S. employment there has been a lack of vigorous and consistent monitoring and law enforcement (Gaille, 2017). There are a few companies that have achieved a high level of diversity in Management, Sodaxo was named the second-best company for diversity, Marriot was named the twenty-first company for diversity and Starwood Hotel and Resorts Worldwide was named thirty-second by the Diversity Inc (Clevenger & Singh, 2013).

In the study was done of participants comprised of alumni from a major U.S Hospitality and Tourism College who are currently working in the industry, of 150 surveys 77% was female while 23% was male (Clevenger & Singh, 2013). The respondents reported that they thought there was a glass-ceiling at a rate of 45.7% the remaining 8.5% was neutral (Clevenger & Singh, 2013). A concern for the participants was at a rate of 63% was that there were fewer female managers than male managers (Clevenger & Singh, 2013).

Chapter 11

National Government Leadership

Women today were still dramatically underrepresented in elective office in the United States. Although, in the analysis of the article it shows that women are just as likely to get elected as men. That being said women were still few in numbers as candidates in these elections (Aguiar & Redlin, 2014).

    The author looked at the political opportunity structure and the individual candidates' attributes (Aguiar & Redlin, 2014). In the past 20 years the proportion of women have only risen 7.7% in the U.S. Congress (Aguiar & Redlin, 2014). The local level has seen the least impact with female state legislatures only growing from 20.5% in 1993 to 23.7% in 2012 (Aguiar & Redlin, 2014). The author wrote that, "the glacial pace of progress suggests that no one alive today will see women elected to political office in parity to their numbers in the larger positions (Aguiar & Redlin, 2014)."

When women are politically excluded from political office it gives the notion that elective office is not attainable by everyone (Aguiar & Redlin, 2014). Some of the benefits of women being in leadership positions in public office is that women leaders are more likely to build consensus and are less concerned with personal credit (Aguiar & Redlin, 2014). Both men and women with political ambitions face conflict within the family unit but women usually chose their family while men follow their political ambitions (Aguiar & Redlin, 2014).

Women and men see their worthiness differently. Women focus on their experiences and specific accomplishments that qualify them to be a candidate (Aguiar & Redlin, 2014). While men are likely to think that any citizen can be a candidate, the Lawless-Fox two stage theory discusses how women are less likely to perceive themselves fit for office (Clance & Imes, 1978; Clance & O'Toole, 1988). Women who are deemed high achievers and are successful leaders in various industries including business, law, and education (Clance & Imes, 1978; Clance & O'Toole, 1988).
These women still perceived themselves as imposters and wonder if they are good enough and able to do the job (Clance & Imes, 1978; Clance & O'Toole, 1988). Men say that they would work and support to improve women's status in society, but they cannot or will not support the idea of lessening men's (McIntosh, 1988, pg. 3). Democracies remained the best arena for women to have a political future as women struggle in civil society to respond to globalization and democratization (Levenson, 2014). The institution of formal politics has a great influence on and power over women. Women need to organize in movements and participate in formal politics (Levenson, 2014). Women are taken more part in public

office because a political party is formally obliged because of affirmative action measures to increase the numbers of women participating as public representatives in political institutions (Levenson, 2014).

Because women are seen as transformational leaders, they have an advantage in political leadership because leaders with complex moral reasoning are more likely to value goals that go beyond immediate self-interest and to foresee the benefits of actions serving the collective good (Will, 2013). In the North Carolina state legislature, women made up 16% of the Senate and they make up 25% of House of Representatives (Levenson, 2014).

Chapter 12

Science Leadership

Upon examining various memberships of the science academics across Brazil, China, France, and the U.S. according to gender, it was found that women only make up percentage wise between 6% and 14% (Academy of Science of South Africa – ASJ AF, 2016).

This is contrast to Brazilian Science where women made up nearly half (49%) of all production of Brazilian Scientific studies (Academy of Science of South Africa – ASJ AF, 2016). There has been progression in Science but there persists to be a gender gap, even at the fact that around the world half of Doctoral Degrees in Science and Engineering in the United States and Europe belong to women (Valentora, 2017).

Women only accounted for one-fifth of full professors are women (Carnes et. al, 2014). Funding for women varies from men in Brazilian Science, where women obtained more funding at the BRL < 30,000 range whereas men scientists are obtaining funding at higher ranges, at BRL < 120,000 (Valentora, 2017). This is to contrast where there is no significant difference in funding in gender for studies in humanities, engineering, exact and earth sciences, life sciences, and applied social sciences (Valentora, 2017). There are various factors that contribute to women being underrepresented including time out for maternity leave and self-exclusion from competition (Valentora, 2017).

One of the limitations is that the Brazilian system of classification of scientists does not consider maternity leave (four to six months) or any other brakes in career service, which could be some of the reasons for the reduction of women in the higher classification levels at the beginning of their careers (Valentora, 2017). Another reason women may drop out is due to them being in the minority.

In Brazil the political parties have done little to undertake the challenge to stimulate and contribute substantively to the increased political participation for women (Wylie & dos Santos, 2016). At a minimum women's presence will break up the party's structure to "stop functioning exclusively as masculine clubs" (Godinho 1996, pg. 155).

Chapter 13

Sports Leadership

Female enrollment in Sport Management academics was not equivalent to their male peers (Harris, 2015). Sports Management is seen as a degree that prepares students for the sports industry (Harris, 2015). Men comprised 75% of sports management students while women only account for 25% (Harris, 2015).

The NFL reported to have only 28% of women in Management while Major League Baseball had 38% and the National Baseball League and Major League Soccer reported to have 42% women in management (Harris, 2015). This study focused on the perception of female undergraduate sports management students. Female athletic directors believed that gender bias and discrimination play a part in the underrepresentation of women pursuing higher level athletic positions (Voepel, 2017).

The same report 77% of women believed the perception that women cannot lead men is another barrier to their overall success (Voepel, 2017). In sports management women are often in positions that are limited in power. These factors have lent itself to a lack of confidence or feeling inadequate (Voepel, 2017). In the undergraduate study these issues rang true with women stating that they did not feel confident in their ability to do the job. Students also revealed that they were dealing with negative stereotypes associated with the sport, other statements indicate that women feel that the sport is traditionally male dominated (Harris, 2015).

    Long work hours and low salary were also a concern. Despite these barriers women were still excited about their entrance into the sports industry (Harris, 2015).

Chapter 14

Women in Leadership: Their Story

Based on the January 2019 S&P list, women currently held 24 (4.8%) of CEO positions (Catalyst, 2019). Women from all career types have faced underrepresentation in leadership positions. One-on-one interviews were done to examine the challenges and barriers women who obtained leadership positions faced during their career journey, and how they overcame the challenges.

The career trail of top-level female leaders was followed to learn what they did to earn a leadership position, their educational background and leadership skills that contributed to the success.

The Board Member – Her Faith

It was an event that was full of excitement and enthusiasm for the upcoming school year and The Board member was one of the speakers for the event. She went around very congenial and talked to the different tables and shook hands. The place was packed but you can tell that the board member was very comfortable in this setting. She began her presentation; her energy was very pleasant but decisive. As she gives directions, everyone is listening very attentive. She walks around and helps and instructs, you can see that is from years of being a teacher. As she goes around and asks questions at every table to see if everyone understood the questions. She continuously monitors the room. Everyone at the tables in teams are assisting each other. She gives them a minute before she starts the next part. She lets each table speak, she gives them more direction and everyone responds accordingly.

You can tell that she has the respect of her colleagues and the people and the others at the event. She is confident, pleasant, and humble. Commanding that event is a woman who sits on the board for their local county schools. She said growing up, she wanted to be a lawyer. Being the oldest of her siblings, she was the one in charge of organizing and giving instructions. Without her knowing it, she was being groomed to be a leader.

On a teacher's scholarship, she went to college, having to teach for four years after college or the scholarship would become a loan according to the Scholarship guidelines. Because of the guidelines, she figured that she would complete the four years of teaching, and then go on to do something else, not knowing that she would fall in love with it.

She loved the idea of helping students reach their fullest potential. As she was teaching, she had a woman Principal who started to put her in charge of things around the school. See, the Principal saw something in her that she did not see within herself. This Principal became one of a few of her mentors throughout the board member's career.

This was the start of her putting what she was naturally doing as a child into fruition. Later, the Principal told her that she should consider going into School Administration.

She decided to go into this field of leadership, only able to be successful because she had people who supported her. She then went on to become a school Principal, which led her on to be on the Board. What stuck out in our conversation, is that she never brought into the hype of being a leader and feeling as if she was above anyone. She believes that everyone has a purpose and a job to do, that no one job was bigger or better than the other. She said that she wanted to make sure that people are respected and that she is respectful.

Mentoring was essential in her success. She had two or three mentors that helped her to get to the next level and then the next level. Without their guidance she may not be in the place that she is in today. She is now paying it forward by assisting others who want to go into leadership positions, while reaching out to those she sees leadership qualities in and helping them reach their fullest potential, as her previous boss the woman Principal did for her. As she has felt left out from the "Boys Club," she wanted to create that same environment with women so that they had their own network of women.

In further discussion, the Board member told me at times that she felt that she wasn't good enough, that every time that she got a promotion she would think, "wow me?" She believes that her Faith and it being a part of God's plan is why she is in the position that she is today. Her Mother's Prayers she says have been evident in her life and other family members. The board member continues to say that she tries to be a positive person and to be good to people, but continues to work hard. Believing those factors has brought her to her leadership position today.

Being respectful to everyone, being professional in the way you dress and speak, having high expectations for herself and for others that work with her, communication skills with formal and informal, to recognize others and forming positive relationships, are the characteristics that she felt that led her to this leadership position. In addition, being genuinely concerned for others and getting to know people, always growing, learning and being future oriented are other characteristics of leadership. It wasn't until late in her career that the board member learned about self-care and that she is still learning how to take a break and enjoy a day off.

Leadership doesn't come without sacrifices. She has found dating as something she didn't have much time for. Because she is dedicated to her job, she didn't know how to turn off and go home and relax. She has never been married or had kids. Having started her leadership position in her early 30s, could be a reason she never started a family because she was so focused on her career. Wondering if maybe she has waited too late, but she tries to remain positive. She has finally met someone, but admits that having time is still an issue for her. She would've had more of a social life but believes that maybe it's God's Plan for things to be the way they are.

When it comes to relationships for women in leadership roles, some men think they are too good for them and feel intimidated that she makes more money than them. Women being perceived as difficult to work with is one of the reasons that more women are not in leadership positions. Women not being able to have the time or due to having to take care of their family could be other factors to them not being in leadership positions. Always looking for role models such as Michelle Obama and Kamala Harris, the board member is excited to see the women who are running for Congress.

The City Manager - Support from Others

Her career transgression started after first going to college. After receiving her Master's in Public Administration, she knew she wanted to be in local government. With the lack of diversity in the area that she lived in, she had to get a job outside of her field. After working outside of her field of study for three years, her and her husband both transferred their jobs and moved.

Within a year she had a job working with the city. Within that same time frame, she met someone at a conference who scheduled her for a meeting with the City Manager. While meeting with the City Manager, she made sure to tell him what her goals were. The City Manager, who was a male, assisted her in getting into a management position. After working eight years with the city, she decided it was time to do something different. She went back into the private sector as a Grants Consultant Director. After working in the private sector and traveling for a while, she applied and received the position as Assistant City Manager, returning back to the City Government. One thing that she highlights was that she had people to help her along the way. Both the City Manager and the Mayor of the town she previously worked with in the City

Government called on her behalf before she even interviewed.

She later left that job due to the crime in the area for another City Government position managing six departments. After staying there for three years, yet again she decided she wanted something more of a challenge. She wanted to go someplace that was more diverse as she was the only woman and African American in that position. Through her diverse experience and background, she was able to get a job in NC.

She believes that mentorship played a big part in her ascension to her leadership position. These mentors were men who she felt because it was a "Good Ole Boy" system, that they had to sign off for her to receive these positions, having to deal with discrimination and bias toward her.

When she started her career in her thirties, women who worked with her would get jealous because they didn't receive a position that she did. Some of the women were upset because they thought that she wasn't deserving of the positions even though they didn't check her background or education. Not only women but also men were upset that they didn't get the job over her. Although she has experienced this all of her life, she didn't let it stop her. Knowing her worth, she persevered through it all, surrounding herself with a network of people who supported her.

Faith is another element that has helped her along her journey. She that the effect that the bias and discrimination had on her made her stronger it made her stand up for herself and it motivated her to keep on pushing. She used any anger that she felt in a positive way. She talks about at times even though she worked harder than a lot of her counterparts who were males or did more work she would at times go unrecognized which she would then speak up for herself. She feels that this deters women from seeking these leadership positions due to them no wanting to deal with it. She said it was a female mentor that she worked with. She feels that she obtained a leadership position while other women who were not able to, was due to her persistence.

  The characteristics that she felt that led her to her leadership position she said due to her management skills, being able to lead people and her leadership skills. Being able to manage people to the best of their abilities. The City Manager believes that her experiences have given her a sensibility to manage others. Communication skills is also key. She said that there were men in her department that didn't want to deal with certain situations where she was open to do so.

  The City Manager thinks that a lot of her leadership skills came from earlier on in Church and learning how to speak in from others there. She feels that everyone of her experiences and jobs have prepared her for her current leadership role. She has sacrificed time with her family and going to see her family back home due to work obligations. Due to this her daughter doesn't really know her side of her family. She worked hard and she said that growing up that she didn't want to be a statistic so she graduated High School at 16 years of age and went on to college away from home because there was not a lot going on in her city.

She thinks that the reason women are not represented, especially in her field is due to it being traditionally majority of the positions being held by white men. In what she does she feels that women are not seen as leaders because males cannot envision women in those kinds of leadership positions. In her experience she feels that men do not want to take instructions from women. Another issue that presents itself often is that women don't see other women as leaders.

The Leader - Mentorship

As I arrived at the groundbreaking event, there is excitement in the air. You can see the Leader, who is over the committee for the ground breaking event, talking to constituents, looking around to make sure that everything was getting done and ready to start the event. She moves freely through the crowds with confidence. Nearby kids are playing, everyone is congregating, and talking.

The Leader arrives at the podium and People listen as she starts to speak. She acknowledges all of the politicians, etc. Fluent in her speaking, you can tell she has made connections. She now directing others and then doing interviews with ease.

The Leader describes what led to her leadership position as a lot of hard work. She never expected to be in her current leadership role. When she was little, she had two older brothers and was very bossy telling them what to do. Her family was in a career of politics, but she ran away from it. Not liking somethings going on in her community, she tried to enlist people to run for office but couldn't get anybody to run. So, with the support of her family and her brother's nudging, she decided to run for office. She admits that at her age at that time of looking for people to run for office, she usually looked for a man.

The first time she went after a leadership position she didn't get it, but felt that she was more qualified just not in the right crowd. Her second time when she actually ran for office - she won. She believes that it was in her to serve and received a lot of support. Her husband is her biggest supporter. As far as her experience with discrimination goes, she feels that men still consider women as second-class citizens.

She recalls being in a meeting when a gentleman on the Board was talking to all the women like a piece of dirt and nothing was done about it and he got a pass. It was only a year and half later that this same gentleman showed his true being on another issue and then he was finally removed. People protected him but She called him out for being disrespectful in which he turned and became disrespectful to her. There were two other women that he was being disrespectful to one younger trying to stand up for herself but he just dismissed her, while an older woman just hung her head.

People doubted her ability to serve due to her being a woman and having kids to take care of. They said that she didn't have a right to run being that she is a wife and a mother like she didn't have any right to run. She said that with the support of her husband and their family that they made it work. With her children being older at the time, she felt that her timing to run was right. Her children encouraged her to run when it was time for re-election. The Leaders key to making this all work is by having a supportive husband. She states that if your husband does not support you in the leadership position that it will never work. She reiterates that it will never work.

There were many sacrifices of being in leadership with her family being her biggest sacrifice and giving up on having friends. People didn't want to be her friend because they were on a different path but ended up being friends with people who are doing the same thing. She did have her core friends that she trusted and valued their opinions but it's hard. The Leader states that the effect that the bias and stereotyping has had on her as being a woman makes her appreciate her spouse more.

She doesn't fault men for being ignorant because it's the way that they were raised. Older men, especially, she feels they are not going to change, because they don't know how. Even being in Church she felt like a fifth-class citizen. Through it all she never let it stop her. The Leader believes that she had a very strong father who was very opinionated and her mentor. She said that when he raised her, he said that "*she is the best boy that he ever raised.*"

Not wanting a man to ever take advantage of her, His goal in life was for her to be able to walk away if she was in a situation. When she was six years old, her father started a business and taught her how to lead. At the age of 16, she had to learn to take charge due to her mother getting sick. Her father taught her to be nice to everyone *because the man that is sleeping under the bridge could one day be your boss.* Teaching her to be independent and to work hard she was told to always act like a lady. Due to her having a great support system with her husband, she was able to obtain a leadership position when other women were not.

Chapter 15

Overcoming Bias in the Workplace

I worked in an organization where I was a manager on a 4 person shift team and the only woman. Outperforming my other male counterparts, I was still being told that I was not performing during each evaluation. Whenever I questioned the results of my performance evaluations, they responded that I wasn't performing without evidence. While the other three males, who I was outperforming, received satisfactory evaluations, I challenged myself to work even harder.

Regardless of how hard I worked and continued to meet the goals, at the next evaluation I received an unsatisfactory and was told that I wasn't performing, while the males still got satisfactory. After receiving several unsatisfactory performance evaluations, I filed a complaint with the EEOC (Equal Employment Opportunity Commission), for discrimination.

That action led to my termination.

The EEOC gave me a right to sue letter in which I did and was awarded $450,000 in District Court after 5 weeks of trial. They appealed the award and then we went to my state Supreme Court where they overturned it. One of the Judges was a woman who is now running for office. "ONCE AGAIN, WE DO IT TO OURSELVES SOMETIMES [as women]."

Women have to overcome bias in the workplace in order to obtain a leadership position (Table 1). Women in the study found that some of the bias that they saw were people feeling as if they didn't deserve the position because they were a woman, feeling left out of the Boy's Club, and being disrespected by men. Eagly and Karau (2002) found that women who are leaders are perceived in a less positive manner when compared to male leaders.

The "old boy network" referred to an informal system of friendships and connections through which men use their positions of influence by providing favors and information to help other men (Nelson, 2017). Outdated male model that shuts women out are based on the "qualities" of a leader — as well as the path to achieve leadership roles — were still largely based on an outdated male model that shuts women out (Ferry, 2020).
One woman from an interview I conducted stated, "I was the Assistant Director and my Director treated me like I was the Administrative Assistant. All of the pats on the back stuff he took ownership, while the grunt work was on me."

The barriers that women face as they try to obtain leadership positions have left some not willing or wanting to endure that, along with wanting to have a family. The women in this study knew that there were barriers to obtaining a leadership position, but they did not let it stop them. They worked extra hard and were very resilient. They recognized the bias that was there but did it anyway. When interviewed the answers that were continuously coming up included participants feeling passed over for jobs due to being a woman, feeling disrespected by mean, and others feeling that they were not deserving of their positions.

Table 1
Overcame bias in the workplace to obtain a leadership position (from interviewees).

Number	Bias
2	Not recognized for leadership position
	Hard work unrecognized
	Passed over for jobs due to gender
3	Felt left out of the boy's club
8	Disrespected by men
10	People feeling that they didn't deserve a promotion

Chapter 16

Personal Sacrifices Made to Obtain Leadership Positions

Growing up and even to this day I never had a lot of friends. I kept my circle close and was never really that sociable. When I was in high school, I didn't even attend proms because I was just that focused on work. And there is absolutely nothing wrong with doing those things but I also knew that those things were distractions and could also possibly derail me from my goal.

My sacrifice always came more from what I could have done in life but because of certain expectations, I chose to take a different path than most. So, while most young women in their twenties were getting married and having kids - that wasn't my focus. And there is nothing wrong with any of that, but I was more focused on my success. Without regret, I currently do not have any children or have ever been married.

Women in leadership roles described the extensive personal costs associated with holding senior leadership positions (Loeffen, 2016). Loeffen (2016) suggested that women leaders can maintain successful careers but not without sacrifices and often not without a system of support. Being able to devote time to romantic and family relationships was one of the top sacrifices that a woman made (Marcus, 2016).

The life of a leader can look glamorous to people on the outside, but the reality was that leadership required sacrifices – "A leader must give up, going up." – John C. Maxwell, (Adewale, 2014).
We can see from the table below the type of personal sacrifices Women made to obtain leadership positions (Table 2). I heard one woman say that they sacrificed dating because their life was their job and did not know how to turn it off and go home and relax.

She never married or had any kids. Another woman said that she had to sacrifice her family. I had a 24-hour job and that I had to sacrifice not being there for her Husband and Daughter." Someone else said they had to sacrifice their personal relationships, including extra time with their children." The top responses when it came to sacrifices that these women made in life were, family time, social life, and self-care.

Table 2

Women who made personal sacrifices to obtain a leadership position (from interviewees).

Number	Sacrifice
2	Family
	Social Life
	Self-Care
3	Privacy

Chapter 17

Women Overcame Barriers Through Faith in God

Faith is a factor that had bonded all the women together. Faith that was embedded from their childhood was a driving force for their lives and their purpose. Even though the bias or prejudice many of them seen through Faith they knew that it was a higher power looking out for them and with this came purpose which no one could take that away from them.

I grew up in the Church, my Grandfather being a Bishop, my Mother a Minister, and my Aunt and Uncles were Pastors. I had a very strong Faith in God. Knowing that God always had the finally say so, and knowing that those barriers couldn't stop me. I have had some type of challenges in various jobs.

For instance, while interviewing for some positions, the owners based their opinion of me on my looks instead of my education and skills. Other times for various jobs I worked for, When I didn't go along with the program and stood up for myself, I got a lot of backlash and retaliation. It was very frustrating and hurtful but my mom kept saying,

"I'm Praying for you," and that along with my faith kept me strong. I was able to persevere through that.

There were many times that I felt like giving up but because of my Faith in God, I kept going and pushing. Even though I knew I was being mistreated as a woman, God kept me going. I remember an interviewee saying, "My leadership position was truly being strong in faith and that I realized that this was part of my purpose and part of my plan, that was connected to my gifts."

Harnessed in them from childhood, the women felt that they were in the leadership positions that they are in today. Through Faith they felt that this was their destiny and could do anything with it. Leadership based on Faith in God makes fulfilled workers, healthy organizations and for good works (Banks, 2000).

Leaders who have Faith are seen to have the following traits: they have confidence in what they are doing and learned to ignored their critics, they have courage in the war of doubt, fear and discouragement, and they operated within constant change and not lose focus (Furtick, 2015). In Fred Kiel's book, "Return on Character: The Real Reason Leaders and Their Companies Win, concluded that the most successful leadership trait is Character (Kiel, 2015).

The four basic traits that Kiel identified were responsibility, compassion, integrity, and forgiveness. Leaders with character tell the truth and own up to their mistakes. Most importantly, they care about people (Kiel, 2015).

Kiel went on to identify those good traits which are listed in the Bible.

Underrepresentation of Women

Chapter 18

Women Overcame Challenges Through Mentorship

Mentorship has been one of the keys for being successful in your career or goals. This theme of mentorship came up multiple times as I interviewed the different women in leadership positions. The Board member who you read about in the chapters above stated, "Mentoring was essential to my success." Others mentioned how their mothers or fathers' advice was essential to their success. I can recall one interviewee stated that "they had the same professional mentor for 12 years, who supported me."

Personally, I have had a few mentors in my life. My first being my mom and family. Ever since I was child, they always encouraged me to go after what I believed, never making me feel as if I couldn't do anything. To this day, they have always supported my endeavors.

When I was at Hampton University, my mentor at the time was the Dean of Entrepreneurship, and I was her student. She was on fire, and brilliant. Being around her, I always said to myself I'm going to be like her one day.

The biggest lessons I learned from my mentors was not about what they said but by the lives that they lived. Their life displayed lessons of perseverance through obstacles, standing firm, being resilient, knowing your stuff, and not taking mess from no one.

The power of mentorship can be overlooked by those who attempt to achieve success on their own. Mentorship is a relationship between two people in which the mentor is usually experienced and can provide "technical & psychological support (Gipson et al., 2017)." All of the women that I interviewed, contested to the fact that it was in part to mentorship by both men and women that they are where they are today.

Executive coaching, mentorship, multi rater feedback, and networking were shown that could assist women in leadership development. (Gipson et. al, 2017). According to Insala (2018a), many women "have broken through the barriers and faced these challenges head-on to obtain top positions."

The author attributes this advancement to the power of mentoring." Being that women often face with challenges that they did not know how to overcome which makes it important to have mentor opportunities (Turner-Moffatt, 2019).

Chapter 19

Women Overcame Challenges Through Family Support

Family support and influence was an element that emerged while studying Women in Leadership. Family played a part because many of them being brought up to fight and to power on with the support of their family, they knew through it all that anything was possible. My Mom and my family have always been my biggest supporters even if I am up or down. They have always been in my corner. Been a shoulder to lean on, cry on, talk to or whatever.

For that I am grateful because I know that everyone wasn't as fortunate as I. One woman who I interviewed stated, "My parents were big on fighting for rights so that made me have a powerful voice because my father made me speak up." Out of only about one-in-five women that was surveyed by the Pew Research Center said that family responsibilities are a major reason there aren't more females in top leadership positions in business and politics (Pew Research Center, 2020).

Another take on this is that family upbringing has a lot to do with leadership. Early family life affected how leaders respond to pressure and react when team members compete for their attention. It influenced whether they have close or distant relationships with the people who reported to them, communicated directly or indirectly, micromanaged or empowered, encouraged debates or shut them down (Jones, 2016).

     Perveen (2013) conducted a content analysis of eight essays relating to women career, professional identity, and work and family balance and found that women who had the support of their family and their employer institutions were better at maintaining a balance between work and family in comparison to those who did not have this support.

Chapter 20

Women Overcoming Barriers Due to their Characteristics

The characteristics of a leader are very important (Table 3). Pew Research stated that 66 percent of women said that being compassionate is critical to being a successful leader, while only 47 percent of men agreed (Pew Research Center, 2020). As far as positive relationships, positive, energizing connections to others were vital to resilience. They provided socio-emotional support, a sense of belonging, and people to share experiences and ideas with (Valcour, 2017).

A good communicator, resilience, and being a team player were listed as top traits of great leaders (Hasan, 2019). I have always thought my greatest characteristic was being resilience. I have been down a thousand times but I always get backup. And when I got backup, I was even better. Something in me will not allow me to give up.

Through gender discrimination, bias, sexual harassment, I kept going and pushing. It takes a special kind of courage to look adversity in the eye and do it anyways. It's definitely not for the faint at heart. But these women believed in themselves and who they were, and they never faltered from that. If one does not believe in themselves and know their worth, they could never be anyone's leader because they are not the leader in their own lives.

Gaining new knowledge about women's experiences with gender bias, role stereotypes and any other obstacles may have assisted current and future generations of women aspiring to leadership positions.

Table 3

Women in leadership who overcame barriers due to their personality traits (from interviewees).

Number	Trait
5	**Hard Working**
3	**Good Listener**
2	**Team Player**
2	**Professional Dress**
2	**Empathetic**
2	**Good**
2	**Always Growing**
2	**Problem Solver**
6	**Resiliency**
2	**Maintain Balance**
2	**Positive Attitude**

Chapter 21

Recommendations to Leaders and Practitioners

The recommendations are being made in order to give organizations and others awareness and guidelines on how to try to overcome barriers for women in leadership.

The first recommendation is for gender sensitivity training within the organization. Women are sometimes seen as second class or less than their male counterparts, and which could be done without even knowing it. By having sensitivity training allows for employees to be made aware of such things. Gender sensitivity training could allow women to feel more comfortable in an organization. A second recommendation is to have a daycare program set up at the office so that would lessen the load for some women.

One of the things that was discussed in the interviews was that some women did not have the support to be able to go to work due to them having to be home with the kids. By having daycare, it gives women the opportunities to explore positions and to be in the workplace, giving them opportunities that they may not have had before.

A third recommendation is to be opened to embracing faith-based programs in the organization. Since the study showed that a lot of the women interviewed said that faith was important to their accession to leadership, faith-based programs could help support them in the workplace. Whenever they are going through things in a workplace, this type of program could give them an outlet to go too.

A fourth recommendation is to have mentorship programs at the organizations. The participants listed that having mentors played a part in them receiving leadership positions.
Mentorship for women is incremental because women usually have fewer mentors in the workplace than their male counterparts. These mentors will be there to assist with passing through the pitfalls and hurdles that will come.

A fifth recommendation was to create a family friendly workplace centered on employee wellbeing. Being that women usually have kids, this will help them to feel supported and not shamed for having a family.

The last and sixth recommendation was to develop a leadership development programs exclusively for women. Like a mirroring effect, women need to see what is possible and see themselves as leaders. Women usually don't see other women in higher level positions. Without that example some women may not believe it's possible to achieve. So, these kinds of programs are needed to nurture and develop the gifts of leadership.

Table 4

Recommendations to Leaders and Practitioners

Theme	Recommendation
Overcoming bias in the workplace to obtain a leadership position	Have gender sensitivity training within the organization.
Women made personal sacrifices to obtain leadership positions	Have a daycare program set up at the office so that would lessen the load for some women
Women in leadership overcame barriers through faith in God	Be opened to embracing faith-based programs in the organization.
Women in leadership overcame challenges through mentorship	Have mentorship programs at the organizations
Women in leadership overcame challenges through family support	Create a family friendly workplace centered on employee wellbeing.
Women in leadership overcame barriers due to characteristics such as being hardworking, resilient, and a good listener	Development programs exclusively for women

Chapter 22

Recommendations for Future Research

More studies are needed to be done on the underrepresentation of women in leadership positions. There was a lack of information pertaining to this topic. More research is needed in the field of mentorship because it seemed to have had a positive effect on the women who were in leadership positions. More mentorship programs in businesses, and more women who were in leadership seeking women how to aspire to be where they were at.

Women had to be able to see what is possible, there are gaps in leadership literature for women that show either improvements or failures of women aspiring to leadership positions in the last decade. Due to the underwhelming number of women who are in leadership positions that some may not deem it of importance to write about (Dvorak, 2015).

"Women remain hugely underrepresented at positions of power in every single sector across the country," said Barnard College president Debora Spar at a White House conference on urban economic development a couple of years ago (Dvorak, 2015 pp.2).

"We have fallen into what I call the 16 percent ghetto, which is when if you look at any sector, be it aerospace engineering, Hollywood films, higher education, or Fortune 500 leading positions, women max out at roughly 16 percent," Spar said. "That is a crime, and it is a waste of incredible talent." (Dvorak, 2015 pp.2)

In the 1970s, women made great strides in the rights sector but progress for women in leadership has plateaued since, and the lack of literature backs this up (Dvorak, 2015). The recession has given corporations excuses not to make efforts to develop women's leadership, particularly in the corporate world (Dvorak, 2015).

The corporate world is where diversity initiatives were often seen as an optional luxury whose budgets were the first to be slashed when financial cutbacks were imposed (Dvorak, 2015).

There is not enough literature available on how to rectify this issue of underrepresentation of women in leadership positions. There is literature on how women are underrepresented and what may and could be causes of this. However, there is not a lot of literature on how to change this perception of why women are not taken serious as leaders and moving forward to make a change (Eagly and Karau, 2002).

The last recommendation for future research is about women in leadership to see what separates the women who have made it compared to the ones who have not as of yet.

There were many reasons it seemed that women were not represented in leadership positions. Through the women that were interviewed, the perception is that biases existed, but that through the themes that were mentioned this gave the women the fortitude to push forward.

Women felt that biases existed but that they were making some strides. From their perception it was also that some women did not want to be in leadership positions due to having to deal with bias and having to sacrifice family time. The women were groomed since children to be leaders without even knowing. Some of this is attributed to their family and background plus their strong faith.

A realization was that through this study that everyone is not cut out to be a leader, but women have a harder time achieving the positions. Women need to be groomed, mentored, and want to sacrifice to even be in the running while men may not have to work that hard but none of these women used that as an excuse. It is my hope as a researcher that the findings might be used by women in order to successfully advance in their aspirations toward leadership positions.

References

American Association of University Women (2016). *Barriers and bias: The status of women in leadership.* https://www.aauw.org/resources/research/barrier-bias/

Academy of Science of South Africa-ASSAF (2016). *Women for science: inclusion and participation in academies of science.* Pretoria. http://www.assaf.org.za/index.php?option=com_content&view=article&id=254:w omen-underrepresented-in-world-science-report-finds&catid=20:assaf- news&Itemid=116

Adewale, A. (2014). *Sacrifice is the heart of leadership.* Brand Development Entrepreneurship.

Aguiar, G., & Redlin, M. (2014). Women's continued underrepresentation in elective office. Great Plains Research; Lincoln, 24(2), 169-179, https://www.jstor.org/stable/44685180

Aguilera, R., Rupp, D., Williams, C., & Ganapathi, J. (2007). Putting the s back in corporate social responsibility: A multilevel theory of social change in organizations. *The Academy of Management Review, 32(3),* 836-863. doi:10.2307/20159338

Akutagawa, L., Deltaas, & Spriggs, S. (2019). *Missing pieces report: The 2018 board diversity census of women and minorities on fortune 500 boards.* Fortune. https://corpgov.law.harvar.edu/2019/02/05/missing-pieces-report-the-2018-board- diversity-census-of women-and-minorities-on-fortune-500-boards.

American Psychological Association (2017). *Summary report, graduate study in psychology 2017: Student Demographics*

Andersen, J., & Hansson, P. (2011). At the end of the road? On differences between women and men in leadership behavior. *Leadership and Organization, Volume 32(5),* 428-441, https://www.emerald.com/insight/content/doi/10.1108/01437731111146550/full/h tml?fullSc=1

Alliance for Board Diversity. (2010). Missing pieces: Women and minorities on Fortune500 boards: 2010 Alliance for Board Diversity census. *Alliance for Board Diversity.*

APA Center for Workforce Studies. (2014a). *Demographic characteristics of APA members by membership characteristics, 2014.* http://www.apa.org/workforce/publications/14-member/profiles.pdf

American Hotel and Lodging Association. (2011). *Lodging industry profile 2010.*
http://www.ahla.com/content.aspx?id=3050

Angel, R., Killacky, J., & Johnson, P, (2013). African-American women aspiring to the superintendency: lived experiences and barriers. *Journal of School of Leadership, 23(4),* 592-614, https://journals.sagepub.com/doi/abs/10.1177/105268461302300402

Badura, K., Grijaiva, E., Jeon, G., Newman, D., & Yan, T. (2018). Gender and leadership Emergence: A meta-analysis and explanatory model. *Personnel Psychology,* 2(1), 66-68. https://onlinelibrary.wiley.com/doi/abs/10.1111/peps.12266

Bailyn, L. (2003). Academic careers and gender equity: Lessons learned from MIT. *Gender, Work and Organization. Gender, Work, and Organization, 10(2),* 137– 153, https://onlinelibrary.wiley.com/doi/abs/10.1111/1468-0432.00008

Baker, D., Larson, L., & Surapaneni, S. (2005). Leadership intentions of young women. The direct and indirect effects of social potency. *Journal of Career Assessment, 24(4)*, 718- 731. https://journals.sagepub.com/doi/abs/10.1177/1069072715616124

Baker, D. (2013). Teaching for gender difference. *National Association for Research in Science 66(3), 78-89, https://onlinelibrary.wiley.com/doi/abs/10.1002/(SICI)1098-237X(199706)81:3%3C259::AID-SCE1%3E3.0.CO;2-C*

Balgiu, B. (2013). Perception of women as managers. The difference of attitudes between employees and non-employees. *Procedia- Social and Behavioral Sciences, 78(1)*, 330-334, https://www.sciencedirect.com/science/article/pii/S1877042813008744

Banks, R. (2000). *Faith in leadership: How leaders live out their faith in their work – and why it matters.* Jossey-Bass, 1st Edition

Bass, B. (1981). *Stogdill's handbook of leadership* (rev. ed.) New York: Free Press

Bedi G, Van Dam NT, & Munafo M. 2012. Gender inequality in awarded research
grants. *Lancet,* 380(9840), 74, https://www.thelancet.com/journals/lancet/article/PIIS0140-6736(12)61292- 6/fulltext

Bellenger, M. (2013). *The glass ceiling vs. the glass escalator.* http://www.women-empowered.com

Belmont Report (2019). *Ethical principles and guidelines for the protection of human subjects of research.* https://www.hhs.gov/ohrp/regulations-and-policy/belmont-report/index.html

Bilimoria, D., & Piderit, S. K. 1994. Board committee membership: Effects of sex-based bias. *Academy of Management Journal, 37(1),* 1453–1477, https://journals.aom.org/doi/abs/10.5465/256795

Blackburn, K. (2017). *The Ceiling versus the escalator.* Penn State

Bobrowski, P., Hoss, M., McDonagh, K., Paris, N., & Schulte, M. (2014). The Leadership gap: ensuring effective healthcare leadership requires inclusion of women at the top. *Open Journal of Leadership, 3(1),* 20-29, https://www.scirp.org/html/2-2330052_46384.htm?pagespeed=noscript

Buchanan, F., Warning, R., & Tett, R. (2012). Trouble at the top: Women who don't want to work for a female boss. *Journal of Business Diversity, 12 (1), 23-34.* http://www.na-businesspress.com/JBD/buchanan_abstract.html

Business Dictionary (2014). *Leadership.* http://www.BusinessDictionary.com.

Burke, R. J. (1984). Mentors in organizations. *Group and Organization Studies,* 9, 353- 372, https://journals.sagepub.com/doi/abs/10.1177/105960118400900304

Cambridge Dictionary, (2013). *Discrimination.*

http://www.CambridgeDictionaryOnline.com.

Carnes, M., Eve, F., Handelsman, J., Pribbenow, C., & Sheridan, J., (2014). Searching for excellence & diversity: Increasing the hiring of women faculty at one academic medical Center. *U.S. National Library of Medicine National Institutes of Health 67(1), 56-78,* https://www.ncbi.nlm.nih.gov/pmc/articles/PMC4128022/

Caryle, T. (1841). *Heroes, hero-worship and the heroic in history.* Bison Book, University of Nebraska Press, Lincoln, NE

Catalyst, (2012). *2012 Fortune 500 board seats and executive officer positions by region.* http://www.catalyst.com

Catalyst, (2017). *Women ceos of the S&P 500.* Retrieved September 10, 2020 from: http://www.catalyst.org/knowledge/women-ceos-sp-500

Catalyst, (2019). Women ceos of the S&P 500. https://www.catalyst.org/knowledge/women-sp-500-companies

Chan, K., & Drasgow, F. (2001). Toward a theory of individual differences and leadership: Understanding the motivation to lead. *The Journal of Applied Psychology, 86,* 481–498, https://psycnet.apa.org/buy/2001-06715-011

Chapman, S. (2018). *The Manufacturing industry is improving its gender diversity.* https://www.manufacturingglobal.com/ai-and-automation/manufacturing- industry-improving-its-gender-diversity-except-leadership-roles

Chen, E. W.-C., & Hune, S. (2011). *Chapter 8: Asian American pacific islander women from Ph. D. to campus president: Gains and leaks in the pipeline.*

In G. Jean-Marie & B. Lloyd-Jones (Eds.), *Women of color in higher education: Changing directions and new perspectives* 10(1), 163–190, https://www.emerald.com/insight/content/doi/10.1108/S1479-3644(2011)0000010012/full/html

Chen, V. (2012). *Powerful women are not helping other women, says study.* http://www.thecareerist.com

Chenail, R. J. (1995). *Presenting qualitative data.* The Qualitative Report. https://nsuworks.nova.edu/cgi/viewcontent.cgi?article=2061&context=tqr#:~:text=Presenting%20Qualitative%20Data%20by%20Ronald%20J.%20Chenail%20.,fo rm%20of%20a%20paper%20or%20a%20lecture.%20The

Cherry, K. (2013). *Lewin's leadership styles: Three major styles of leadership.* http://www.abouteducation.com

Cherry, K. (2018). Transformational leadership. A closer look at the effects of transformational leadership. *Very Well Mind,* 4(1), 16-24, https://www.verywellmind.com/what-is-transformational-leadership-2795313

Chesterman, C, Ross-Smith, A, & Peters, M (2005) Not doable jobs! Exploring senior women's attitudes to academic leadership roles. *Women's Studies International Forum* 28(1), 163–180, https://journals.sagepub.com/doi/abs/10.1177/1350506810377407

Christnacht, C., & Laughlin, L. (2017). *Women in manufacturing.* https://www.census.gov/newsroom/blogs/random-samplings/2017/10/women- manufacturing.html

Clance, P. & Imes, S. (1978). The impostor phenomenon in high achieving women: dynamics and therapeutic interventions. *Psychotherapy: Theory Research and Practice 15(1)*, 241-47. https://psycnet.apa.org/journals/pst/15/3/241/

Clance, P., & O'Toole, M. (1988). The imposter phenomenon: An internal barrier to empowerment and achievement. *Women and Therapy 6(1)*, 51-64.

Korean J Med Educ., 29 (2), 61-71, https://www.ncbi.nlm.nih.gov/pmc/articles/pmc5465434/

Clevenger, L., Singh, N. (2013). Exploring barriers that lead to the glass ceiling effect for women in the U.S. hospitality industry. *Journal Human Resources in Hospitality of Tourism, 12(4)*, 376-399, https://www.tandfonline.com/doi/abs/10.1080/15332845.2013.790258

Cohen, D. (2018). *Women minorities are still underrepresented on the boards of social media and tech companies.* https://www.adweek.com/digital/women-minorities- are-still-underrepresented-on-the-boards-of-social-media-and-tech-companies/

Deane, C., Morin R. (2016). *Women and leadership. Public says women are equally qualified, but barriers persist.* https://www.pewsocialtrends.org/2015/01/14/women-and-leadership/

Deloitte, (2013). *Untapped Resource: How manufacturers can attract, retain, and advance talented women.*

https://www2.deloitte.com/content/dam/Deloitte/us/Documents/manufacturing/us-indprod-pip-women-in-manufacturing-report-02052013.pdf

Dvorak, P. (2015). *DC is run by women leaders. Time for the rest of\America to catch up.* Chicago Tribune https://www.chicagotribune.com/news/opinion/commentary/sns-wp-washpost-bc- district-women-comment05-20150105story.html

Eagly, A., & Johnson, B. (1990). Gender and leadership style: A Meta-Analysis. *Psychological Bulletin, 108*(2), 235-256, https://psycnet.apa.org/doiLanding?doi=10.1037/0033-2909.108.2.233

Eagly, A., & Karau, S. (2002*).* Role congruity theory of prejudice toward female leader*s. Psychological Review, 109*(3), 573-598, https://psycnet.apa.org/buy/2002-13781-007

Eagly, A., & Carli, L. (2007). *Through the labyrinth: The truth about how women become leaders.* Boston, MA: Harvard Business School Press.

Eagly, A., Johannesen-Schmidt, M., & van Engen, M. (2003). Transformational, transactional, and laissez-faire leadership styles: A meta-analysis comparing women and men. *Psychological Bulletin*, 129, 569-591. 10.1037/0033-2909.129.4.569

Equality Challenge Unit (2015a) *Equality in higher education: statistical report 2015 Part 1.* https://www.advance-he.ac.uk/knowledge-hub/equality-higher-education- statistical-report-2015

Elprana, G., Felfe, J., Stiehl, S., & Gatzka, M. (2015). Exploring the sex difference in affective motivation to lead. Furthering the understanding of women's underrepresented in leadership positions. *Journal of Personal Psychology. 14(3),*142-152, https://econtent.hogrefe.com/doi/full/10.1027/1866-5888/a000137

Ely, R. (1994). The effects of organizational demographics and social identity on
relationships among professional women. *Administrative Science Quarterly, 39(1),* 203-238, https://www.jstor.org/stable/2393234

Ely, R. J. (1995). The power in demography: Women's social constructions of gender identity at work. *Academy of Management Journal,* 38(1), 589-634. 10.1037/0021-9010.82.3.342

England, P. (1992). *Comparable worth: theories and evidence.* Routledge; 1st Edition Epstein, C. F. (1970). Woman's place. Berkeley, CA: University of California Press. *Annals of the New York Academy of Sciences* 208(1), 62-70, https://journals.sagepub.com/doi/abs/10.1177/016001760002300201

Eurydice (2012). *Entrepreneurship, education at school in Europe.*
https://www.europarl.europa.eu/greece/resource/static/files/enter pre neurship-education-at-school-in-europe.pdf

European University Association (2017). *Female university leadership in Europe.*

European University Association. https://epws.org/female-university-leadership- europe/

Evans, G. (2001). Play like a man, win like a women: What men know about success that women need to learn. Crown Business Freeman, S., & Varey, R. (1997).

Women communicators in the workplace: Natural born marketers? *Marketing Intelligence & Planning,* 15 (7), 318-32, https://www.emerald.com/insight/content/doi/10.1108/02634509710193163/full/h tml

Federal Glass Ceiling Commission. (1995). *Executive summary: Fact finding report of the federal glass ceiling.* http://www.dol.gov/oasam/programs/history/reich/reports/ceiling1.pdf.

Ferry, K. (2020). *Barriers & Bias: The status of women in leadership.* https://www.aauw.org/resources/research/barrier-bias/

Fielder, F. (1964). *A theory of leadership effectiveness. In L. Berkowitz (Ed.), Advances in experimental social psychology.* New York, NY: Academic Press.

Forsyth, D. (2014). *Group dynamics (6th ed.).* USA: Wadsworth Cengage Learning. 978-0-495-59952-4.

Francis, J.J., Johnston, M., Robertson, C., Glidewell, L., Entwistle, V. Eccles, M. P., & Grimshaw, J. M. (2010). What is an adequate sample size? Operationalizing data saturation for theory-based interview studies. Psychology and Health, 25(10), 1229-1245. https:doi:10.1080/08870440903194015

Freeman, S., & Varey, R. (1997). Women communicators in the

workplace: Natural born marketers? *Marketing Intelligence & Planning, 15*(7), 318-24, https://www.emerald.com/insight/content/doi/10.1108/02634509710193163/full/h tml

Gaile, B. (2017). *17 Hospitality Industry Employment Statistics.* https://brandongaille.com/15-hospitality-industry-employment-statistics/

Galton, F. (1869). *Hereditary Genius.* Ostara Publications

Gaeun, S., Wenhao, H., & Seung-Hyun, C. (2017). Conceptual review of underrepresentation of women in senior leadership positions from a perspective of gendered social status in the workplace. *Implications for HRD Research & Practice*

Gluck, S. (2014). *The effects of gender discrimination in the workplace.* http://www.DemandMedia.com

Gipson, A., Pfaff, D., Mendelsohn, D, Catenacci, L., & Burke, W. (2017). Women on leadership, selection, development, leadership style, and performance. *The Journal of Applied Science,* https://journals.sagepub.com/doi/abs/10.1177/0021886316687247

Goodman, J. S., Fields, D. L., & Blum, T. C. (2003) Cracks in the glass ceiling: In what kinds of organizations do women make it to the top? *Group & Organization Management, 28(4),* 475-501, https://journals.sagepub.com/doi/abs/10.1177/1059601103251232

Godinho T. (1996). Ação afirmativa no partido dos trabalhadores

. *Estudos Feministas 4(1),* 148, https://periodicos.ufsc.br/index.php/ref/article/download/16664/15233

Graen, G., & Uhl-Bien, M. (1995). *Relationship-based approach to leadership: Development of leader-member exchange (LMX) theory of leadership over 25 years: Applying a multi-level multi-domain perspective.* University of Nebraska Management Department Faculty Publication, https://www.sciencedirect.com/science/article/pii/1048984395900365

Grant, T. (2016). *Women in business: Turning promise into practice.* http://www.grantthornton.global/globalassets/wib_turning_promise_into_practice.

Gregor, M., & O'Brien, K. (2015). The changing face of psychology. Leadership Aspirations of Female Doctoral Students. *The counseling psychologist, 43(8),* 1090-1113, https://journals.sagepub.com/doi/abs/10.1177/0011000015608949

Gregory-Mina, H. (2012). Gender barriers of women striving for a corporate officer Position: A Literature Review. *Advancing Women in Leadership*, 1093(1099), 54-78, https://awl-ojs-tamu.tdl.org/awl/index.php/awl/article/view/87

Grow, J., & Mensa, M. (2015). *Creative women in Peru: Outliers in a machismo world.* Universidad de Navarra, https://epublications.marquette.edu/comm_fac/414/

Haines, E. L., Deaux, K., & Lofaro, N. (2016). The times they are a-changing. . . or are they not? A comparison of components of gender stereotypes, 1983 to 2014. *Sex Roles*, 40(1), 353–363, 10.1177/0361684316634081

Handelsman J, Cantor N, Carnes M, Denton D, Fine E, Grosz B, Hinshaw V, Marrett C, Rosser S, Shalala D, & Sheridan J (2005). More women in science. *Science 309(5738),* 1190-1191, https://science.sciencemag.org/content/309/5738/1190.summary

Harris, K., Grappendorf, H. Aicher, T., & Veraldo, C. (2015). Discrimination? Low pay? Long hours? I am still excited: Female sport management students' perceptions of barriers toward a future career in sport. *Advancing Women in Leadership, 35(21),* 10, https://awl-ojs-tamu.tdl.org/awl/index.php/awl/article/view/128

Hillman, A. J., Cannella, A. A., & Harris, I. C. 2002. Women and racial minorities in the boardroom: How do directors differ? *Journal of Management*, 28(1), 747–763, https://journals.sagepub.com/doi/abs/10.1177/014920630202800603

Hirsch, E. (2002). *The new dictionary of cultural literacy* (Third Edition). Houghton Mifflin Company.

Holiday, E., & Rosenberg, J. (2009). *Girls, meaner women: Understanding why women backstab, betray, and trash-talk each other and how to deal.*

Orchid Press, Central, Hong Kong Hopkins, M. M., O'Neil, D. A., Passarelli, A., & Bilimoria, D. (2008). Women's leadership development strategic practices for women and organizations. *Consulting Psychology Journal: Practice and Research*, 60(1), 348-365, https://psycnet.apa.org/record/2008-17523-007

Hull, R., Umansky, P. (1997). An Examination of gender stereotyping as an explanation for vertical job segregation in public accounting. *Organizational & Society*. 22(1), 507-528, https://www.sciencedirect.com/science/article/pii/S0361368296000281

Hums, M. A. (1994). Successful recruitment and retention of minority students in sport management. *Women in Sport and Physical Activity Journal*, 5(2), 10.1123/wspaj.5.2.89

Ibarra, H., & Obodaru, O. (2009). Women and the vision thing. *Harvard Business Review, 87* (1), 62-70, http://storage.ugal.com/3066/womenthe-vision-thing.pdf

Ibarra, H., Carter, N., & Silva, C. (2010). Why men still get more promotions than women. *Harvard Business Review, 88*(9), 80-126, https://archive.bio.org/sites/default/files/docs/toolkit/Why%20Men%20Still%20G et%20More%20Promotions%20than%20Women_HBR%20article.pdf

Insula (2018). *Empowering women leaders with mentoring.* https://www.insala.com/blog/empowering-women-leaders-through-mentoring

Jackson, J. C. (2001). Women middle managers' perception of the glass ceiling. *Women in Management Review, 16*(1), 30-41, https://www.emerald.com/insight/content/doi/10.1108/09649420110380265/full/h tml

Joppe, M. (2001). *The Research Process.*

http://www.ryerson.ca/~mjoppe/rp.htm

Kanter, R. (1993). *Men and women of the corporation.* BasicBooks, New York, NY.

Kesner, I. F. (1988). Directors' characteristics and committee membership: An investigation of type, occupation, tenure, and gender. *Academy of Management Journal*, 31(1), 66–84, https://journals.aom.org/doi/abs/10.5465/256498

Khaleeli, H. (2011). *Indra Nooji Pepsico's boss is keen to help women and other minorities in the business world up the ladder.* http://www.theguardian.com

Kiene, C. (2016). Nearly two-thirds of mothers are breadwinners, black and Latina mothers more likely to be breadwinners. *Center for American Progress.* https://www.americanprogress.org/wp-content/uploads/issues/2012/04/pdf/breadwinners.pdf

Kiel, F. (2015). *Return on character: The Real reason leaders and their companies win.* Harvard Business Review Press

Kim, D., & Starks, L. (2016). Gender diversity on corporate boards: Do women contribute unique skills. *The American Economic Review: Nashville.* 106(5), 267-271, https://www.aeaweb.org/articles?id=10.1257/aer.p20161032

Kingsley, P. (2011). *Carol Bartz The first female CEO of a major software company.* http://www.theguardian.com

Klenke, K. (2011). *Women in leadership: Contextual dynamics and boundaries.* Bingley,
UK, Emerald Group Publishing.

Klettner, A., Clarke, T., Boersma, M. (2014). Strategic and regulatory approaches to increasing women in leadership: Multilevel targets and mandatory quotas as levers for cultural change. *J. Bus. Ethics 133(1)*, 395-419, https://link.springer.com/article/10.1007/s10551-014-2069-z

Krause, S. (2017). *Leadership: Underrepresentation of women in higher education.*
ProQuest,
https://www.une.edu/sites/default/files/leadership_underrepresentation_of_wome n_in_higher_education.pdf

Kvale, S. (1996). *Interviews: An Introduction to qualitative research intensity.* Thousand Oaks, CA, Sage.

Lamnek, S. (2005). *Qualitative sozialforsching.*

Lehrbuch. 4. Auflage. Beltz Verlay.Weihnhein, Basl, http://archives.un-pub.eu/index.php/P-ITCS/article/viewArticle/3065

Langowitz, N. & Minniti, M. (2007), The entrepreneurial propensity of women, Entrepreneurship. *Theory and Practice*, 31(3), 341-364,
https://journals.sagepub.com/doi/abs/10.1111/j.1540-6520.2007.00177.x

Lapchick, R. E. (2012a). *Racial and gender report card: Major League Soccer.*
University of Central Florida.
http://web.bus.ucf.edu/documents/sport/2012mlsrgrc.pdf

Lapchick, R. E. (2012b). *Racial and gender report card:*

National Football League.
http://www.tidesport.org/RGRC/2012/2012_NFL_RGR_C.pdf

Lapchick, R. E. (2012c). *Racial and gender report card: National Basketball League.* University of Central Florida. http://web.bus.ucf.edu/documents/sport/2012_NBA_RG RC.pdf

Lapchick, R. E. (2013). *Racial and gender report card: Major League Baseball*
http://www.tidesport.org/RGRC/2013/2013_MLB_RGR C_Final_Correction.pdf

Leedy, P., & Ormond, J. (2016). *Planning and design (11th ed.).* Upper Saddle River, NJ:

Pearson. Lemak, C. (2016). *Women in healthcare leadership project.* National Center for Health Care Leadership, https://journals.lww.com/hcmrjournal/fulltext/2018/01000/Hospital_cultural_com petency_as_a_systematic.5.aspx

Levenson, A. (2014). *Women leaders in North Carolina government: We still have a long way to go.* https://onlinempa.unc.edu/women-leaders-north-carolina-government-still-long-way-go/

Lewin, K., Lippit, R., &White, R. (1939). Patterns of aggressive behavior in experimentally created social climates. *Journal of Social Psychology, 10(1),* 271- 299, https://www.tandfonline.com/doi/pdf/10.1080/00224545.1939.9713366

Likert, R. (1976). *New ways of managing conflict.*

McGraw-Hill, New York City, NY LFHE (2015) *Governor's Views of their Institutions, Leadership and Governance.* https://www.advance-he.ac.uk/knowledge-hub/governors-views-their-institutions-leadership-and-governance

Long, C. (2013). *Women, leadership and the "glass cliff": Research Roundup.* https://journalistsresource.org/studies/society/gender-society/women-leadership-glass-cliff-research-roundup/

Longman, K., & Lafreniere, S. (2012). Beyond the stained glass ceiling: Preparing women for leadership in faith-based higher education. *Advancing in Developing Human Resources 14(1)*, 45-61, https://journals.sagepub.com/doi/abs/10.1177/1523422311427429

Lough, N., & Grappendorf, H. (2007). Senior women administrator's perspectives on professional advancement. *International Journal of Sport Management*, 8(1), 193–209, https://www.sciencedirect.com/science/article/pii/S1441352315000479

Lucas, S. (2012). *Beyond the existence proof: Ontological conditions, epistemological implications, and in-depth interview research.* Quality and Quantity, ed. Springer Publications, New York, NY.

Mabokela, R. O. (2003). Donkeys of the university: Organizational culture and its impact on South African women administrators. *Higher Education*, 46(2), 129–145, https://link.springer.com/article/10.1023/A:1024754819125

Madsen, S. (2011). Women and leadership in higher education:

Current realities, colleagues, and future directions. *Advances in Developing Human Resources, 14*(2), 131-139, https://journals.sagepub.com/doi/abs/10.1177/1523422311436299

Mahmood, A. (2015). Home grown female leadership models. *Planning and Changing; Normal* 46(1), 354-380, https://www.homeworkforyou.com/static_media/uploadedfiles/Home%20grown%20female%20leadership%20models.pdf

Manfredi, S, Grisoni, L, Handley, K, Nestor, R, Cooke, F (2014) Gender and higher education leadership: Researching the careers of top management program Alumni. *Management in Education,* 10.1177%2F0892020617696631

Martinez, A.C., Levie, J., Kelley, D.J., Sæmundsson, R.J. & Schøtt, T. (2010). A *Global perspective on entrepreneurship education and training.* https://pureportal.strath.ac.uk/en/publications/global-entrepreneurship-monitor- special-report-a-global-perspecti

Manta, (2013). Companies in North Carolina. http://www.manta.com

Mallia, K.L (2009, October 2). Rare birds: why so few women become ad agency creative directors. *Advertising and Society Review* 10(3). http://muse.jhu.edu/

Masteralexis, L. P., Barr, C. A., & Hums, M. A. (2009). *Principles and practice of sport management.* Sudbury; MA: Jones and Bartlett.

Maume, D. (2004). *Is the glass ceiling a unique form of inequality? Evidence from a random-effects model of managerial attainment*. Sage Publications, Thousand Oaks, CA.

Rishani M., Mallah, M., Houssami, S., & Ismail, H. (2015). Lebanese perceptions of the glass ceiling, *Equality, Diversity and Inclusion: An International Journal,* 34(8), 678-691, https://www.emerald.com/insight/content/doi/10.1108/EDI-11-2014-0082/full/html

McCarthy, N. (2018). *Women are still earning more doctoral degrees than men in the U.S. Forbes.* https://www.forbes.com/sites/niallmccarthy/2018/10/05/women-are-still-earning-more-doctoral-degrees-than-men-in-the-u-s-infographic/#4c6da3d545b6

McComb-DiPesa, L. (2005). *A History of women in industry.* https://www.journals.uchicago.edu/doi/abs/10.1086/211825

McDonald, M., & Westphal, J. (2013). Access denied: How mentoring of women and minority first-time directors and its negative effects on appointments to additional boards. *Academy of Management Journal*, 56(4), 1169-1198, https://journals.aom.org/doi/abs/10.5465/amj.2011.0230

McIntosh, P. (1988). *White privilege and male privilege: A Personal account of coming to see correspondences through work in women's studies.* Working Paper No. *189.* Wellesley College.

McNeill, C. (2018). *3 Reasons to conduct more exploratory research.* https://www.gutcheckit.com/blog/3-reasons-conduct-exploratory-research/

Meek, V. L., Goedegebuure, L., Santiago, R., & Carvalho, T.

(Eds.). (2010). *The Changing dynamics of higher education middle management* (Vol. 33). Dordrecht: Springer.

Mensa, M. (2012). Creativos Publicitarios en el Perú. *Zer 17(33)*, 47-66. Mestechkina, T., Shin, J., Son, N. (2014). *Parenting in Vietnam.*
https://www.researchgate.net/publication/263602221_Argentine_culture_and_par enting_styles
Metz, I., Kulik, C. T. (2014). *The rock climb: Women's advancement in management.* In Kumra, S., Simpson, R., Burke, R. J. (Eds.), *The Oxford handbook of gender in organizations.* New York, NY: Oxford University Press.

Mills, G. (2010). *Action research.* Upper Saddle River, NJ: Pearson.

Minniti, M. , Arenius, P. and Langowitz, N. (2005), *2004 Report on women and entrepreneurship*, Babson College, Wellesley, MA.

Mizrahi, R. (2004). Hostility in the presence of women: Why women undermine each other in the workplace and the consequences for Title VII. *Yale Law Journal, 113(1),* 1579, https://heinonline.org/hol-cgi-bin/get_pdf.cgi?handle=hein.journals/ylr113&section=60

Morley, L (2013) The rules of the game: Women and the leaderist turn in higher education. *Gender and Education, 25(1),* 116–131,
https://www.tandfonline.com/doi/abs/10.1080/09540253.2012.740888

National Partnership (2017). *North Carolina women and the wage gap. National Partnership April 2017.*

www.nationalpartnership.org/our-work/resources/workplace/fair-pay/4-2017-nc-wage-gap.pdf

National Science Foundation, National Center for Science and Engineering Statistics. (2010). *Survey of graduate students and post doctorates in science and engineering.* http://www.nsf.gov/statistics/wmpd/2013/pdf/ tab3-1.pdf

Nayab, N. (2011). *How to determine whether your qualitative research is valid?* http://www.brighthubpm.com

NC Budget Management (2017). *County estimates.* https://www.osbm.nc.gov/demog/county-estimates

Nelson, A. (2017). *Women and the good ole boys club.* https://www.psychologytoday.com/us/blog/he-speaks-she-speaks/201703/women- and-the-good-ole-boys-club

Neuman, W. (2005). *Social research methods: Qualitative and quantitative approaches (6th ed.).* Boston, MA: Allyn & Bacon.

Nguyen, T., & Huong, S. (2013). Barriers to and facilitators of female deans' career advancement in higher education: An Exploratory study in Vietnam. *Higher Education; Dordrecht 66(1),* 123-138, https://link.springer.com/article/10.1007%252Fs10734-012-9594-4

Noland, M, Moran, T, & Kotschwar, B (2016) *Is gender diversity profitable? Evidence from a global survey.* https://www.piie.com/publications/working-papers/gender-diversity-profitable-evidence-global-survey

North Carolina Department of Public Instruction. (2009). *North Carolina public schools statistical profile 2009,*

http://www.ncpublicschools.
org/docs/fbs/resources/data/statisticalprofile/2009profile.pdf

North Carolina Department of Public Instruction. (2011). Statistical profiles and data reports.
http://www.dpi.state.nc.us/data/reports

North Carolina Department of the Secretary of State (2013). Corporations division.
http://www.secretary.state.nc.us/corporations

Oshagbemi, T., & Roger, G. (2003). Gender differences and similarities in the leadership styles and behaviour of UK managers. *Women in Management Review*, 18, 288- 298. doi:10.1108/09649420310491468

Google Scholar, Crossref Ozkanli, O., & White, K. (2008). Leadership and strategic choices: Female professors in Australia and Turkey. *Journal of Higher Education Policy and Management, 30 (1), 53-63,*
https://www.tandfonline.com/doi/abs/10.1080/13600800701745051

Paustian-Underdahl, S., Walker, L. S., & Woehr, J. W. (2014). Gender and perceptions of leadership effectiveness: A meta-analysis of contextual moderators. *Journal of Applied Psychology*, 99, 1129-1145. doi:10.1037/a0036751

Patton, M. (1990). *Qualitative evaluation and research methods (2nd ed.).* Newbury Park, CA: SAGE.

Patton, M. Q. (2001). *Qualitative evaluation and research methods (3rd ed.).* Thousand Oaks, CA: Sage Publications, Inc.

Pohlhaus, J. R., Jiang, H., Wagner, R. M., Schaffer, W. T., Pinn, V. W. (2011). Sex differences in application, success, and funding rates for NIH extramural programs. *Academic Medicine* 86(6), 59-67,
https://www.ncbi.nlm.nih.gov/pmc/articles/pmc3379556/

Potter, J. (2008), *Entrepreneurship and higher education.* http://www.oecd.org/publications/entrepreneurship-and-higher-education- 9789264044104-en htm

Powell, G. N., & Butterfield, D. A. (1989*)*. The "good manager": Did androgyny fare better in the 1980s? *Group and Organization Studies, 14*(2), 216-233,
https://journals.sagepub.com/doi/abs/10.1177/105960118901400209

Powell, G. N. (2014). *Sex, gender, and leadership.* In Kumra, S., Simpson, R., Burke, R.J. (Eds.), *The Oxford handbook of gender in organizations* New York, NY: Oxford University Press.

Quast, L. (2010). *Women helping other women? Not so much, it seems.* from: http://www.forbes.com

Ragins, B., & Cotton, J. (1999). Mentor functions and outcomes: A comparison of men and women in formal and informal mentoring relationships. *Journal of Applied Psychology, 84*(1), 529-550, https://psycnet.apa.org/record/1999-11038-005

Regine, B. (2011). *Why is it That women are seen as less competent*
https://www.forbes.com/sites/85broads/2011/04/14/why-is-it-that-women-are- seen-as-less-competent/#3ba69e7394db

Rivera, T. (2016). *Female superintendents in NC and the U.S* https://www.pbs.org/newshour/education/women-run-nations-school-districts Roesner, J. (1990). *The way women lead.* http://www.hbr.org

Ross, S. (2011). *Leadership development in corporate America. Ann Arbor, MI: Bridgewater State University.* http://digitalcommons.www.na- businesspress.com/Ross.pdf

Saladana, J. (2012). *The coding manual for qualitative researchers.* Thousand Oaks, CA: Sage.

Sapsford, R., & Jupp, V. (2006). *Data collection and analysis* (2nd ed.). SAGE Publications Ltd., Thousand Oaks, CA

Savigny, H (2014) Women, know your limits: Cultural sexism in academia. *Gender and Education 26(7),* 794–809, https://www.tandfonline.com/doi/abs/10.1080/09540253.2014.970977

Scantlebury, K. (2009). *Gender role stereotyping.* http://www.education.com

Schein, V.E. (2000). A Global look at psychological barriers to women's in progress management. *Journal of Social Issues. 57(4), 675-688. DOI:10:1111/0022- 4537.00235*

Schein, V. E. (1973). The relationship between sex role stereotypes and requisite management characteristics. *Journal of Applied Psychology, 57*(2), 95-100, https://psycnet.apa.org/journals/apl/57/2/95/

Schein, V.E. (2015). Think manager-think male? Implications of gender balance. *women at the TOP international scientific conference,* https://www.emerald.com/insight/content/doi/10.1108/09649420710726193/full/html

Schelmetic, T. (2012). *Why more women aren't in manufacturing.* http://www.thomasnet.com

Schilling, N. (2013). *The Coming rise of women in manufacturing.*
https://www.forbes.com/sites/forbeswomanfiles/2013/09/20/the-rise-of-women-in-manufacturing/#282e844a1d98

Schmitt, M. T., Spoor, J. R., Danaher, K., & Branscombe, N. R. (2009). *Rose-colored glasses: How tokenism and comparisons with the past reduce the visibility of gender inequality.* Washington, DC: American Psychological Association.

Scott, W. (1981). *Organizations: rational, national, and open systems.* Englewood Cliffs, NJ: Prentice Hall Inc.

Segal, R. (2000). *Hero myths.* Wiley-Blackwell, Hoboken, NJ

Shapiro, V. (1982) Private costs of public commitments or public costs of private commitments? Family roles versus political ambition. *American Journal of Political Science* 26 (2), 265-79, https://www.jstor.org/stable/2111039

Sharma, R., & Givens-Skeaton, S. (2010). Advancing women in leadership. *Review of Business Research,* 30(1), 1, https://www.emerald.com/insight/content/doi/10.1108/09649420610692534/full/html

Sharma, R., & Givens-Skeaton, S. (2012*).* Gender diversity among leaders of US corporations. *Review of Business Research, 12*(5), 169-176, https://papers.ssrn.com/sol3/papers.cfm?abstract_id=2729348

Shellenbarger, S. (2018). *New strategies help women build*

career Confidence. https://www.wsj.com/articles/women-strive-to-narrow-a-confidence-gap- 1521465138

Shellenbarger, S. (2011). *Why women rarely leave middle management.* https://www.wsj.com/articles/BL-JB-14476

Shepherd, S (2015b*) Appointing deputy and pro vice chancellors in pre-1992 English universities: Managers, management and managerialism.* Unpublished PhD thesis, University of Kent, UK.

Shepherd, S (2014) The rise of the career PVC. *The Leadership Foundation for Higher Education's Engage* (36):10–13. http://www.lfhe.ac.uk/en/research- resources/publications-hub/past-editions/engage-36--autumn-2014/in-practice/index.cfm

Shepherd, S. (2017). Why are there so few female leaders in higher education? A Case of Structure or Agency? *Management in Education.* 31(2), 82-87, https://journals.sagepub.com/doi/abs/10.1177/0892020617696631

Sheppard, L. (2013). *Study finds workplace conflicts between women judged more harshly.* http://www.torontosun.com

Sheppard, L., & Aquino, K. (2012). Much ado about nothing? Observers' problematization of women's same-sex conflict at work. *Academy of Management Perspectives, 27(1),* 52-62, https://journals.aom.org/doi/abs/10.5465/amp.2012.0005

Smith, A. (2015). On the edge of a glass cliff: Women in leadership in public organizations. *Public Administration Quarterly; Randallstown. 39(3),* 484-517, https://www.jstor.org/stable/24773425

Spar, D. (2012). *Women and the leadership gap.* https://electwomen.com/2012/03/women-and-the-leadership-gap/

Stevenson, L. & Lundström, A. (2001), *Patterns and trends in entrepreneurship/SME policy and practice in ten countries.* http://www.africres.org/SMME%20Research/SMME%20Research%20General/ Working%20Papers/PATTERNS%20AND%20TRENDS%20IN%20ENTREPRE NEURSHIPSME%20POLICY%20AND%20PRACTICE%20IN%20TEN%20EC ONOMIES.pdf

Stivers, C. (2002) *Gender images in public administration: legitimacy and the administrative state*, Thousand Oaks, CA: Sage.

Sumer, H. C. (2006). Women in management: Still waiting to be full members of the club. Sex Roles. *A Journal of Research, 55(1/2), 63-72,* https://link.springer.com/article/10.1007/s11199-006-9059-2

Swers, M. L. (2002). *The difference women make.* Chicago: University of Chicago Press.

Tahmincioghu, E. (2010). Women still reluctant to help each other. NBC news. *The Journal of Business Diversity, 12*(1), 33-46, https://journals.sagepub.com/doi/pdf/10.1177/073953290102200202

Tellegen, A., & Waller, N. G. (2008). *Exploring personality through test construction: Development of the Multidimensional Personality Questionnaire.* In Boyle, G. J., https://books.google.com/books?hl=en&lr=&id=sdD41qBTJSUC&oi=fnd&pg=PA261&dq=Exploring+personality+through+test+construction:+Development+of+the+Multidimensional+Personality+Questionnaire&ots=Xm6l8u9U2H&sig=r081RyekNmmLifZ9mX53PNNo8kI

Matthews, G., Saklofske, D. H. (n.d.), *The Sage handbook of personality theory and assessment* (pp. 261–292). Los Angeles, CA: Sage.

The University of Buffalo School of Management, (2019). *Study finds the reason why women are not seen as leaders in the corporate world.* https://timesofindia.indiatimes.com/life-style/relationships/work/study-finds-the-reason-why-women-are-not-seen-as-leaders-in-the-corporate-world/photostory/69725629.cms

The White House Project. (2009). *The White house project report: Benchmarking women's leadership.* http://www.thewhitehouseproject.com

Thomas, G. (2011). Sonia is typing: A typology for the case study in social science following a review of definition,discourse, and structure. *Qualitative Inquiry, 17(6),* 511-521, https://journals.sagepub.com/doi/abs/10.1177/1077800411409884

Thomas, S. (1994). *How women legislate.* New York: Oxford

University Press.

Tickle, L. (2017). *Why universities can't see women as leaders*. The Guardian. www.theguardian.com/higher-education-network/2017/mar/08/why-universities- cant-see-woman-as-leaders

Tilbrook, K. E. (1998). An exploration of the current under-representation of senior women managers in Australian universities. *Women in Management Review, 13(8)*, 291–298, https://www.emerald.com/insight/content/doi/10.1108/09649429810243180/full/h tml

Tlaiss, H.A. (2014), Between the traditional and the contemporary: careers of women managers from a developing Middle Eastern country perspective, *The International Journal of Human Resource Management, 25(20)*, 2858-2880, https://www.tandfonline.com/doi/abs/10.1080/09585192.2014.914054

Tlaiss, H. & Kauser, S. (2010), Perceived organizational barriers to women's career advancement in Lebanon, *Gender in Management: An International Journal*, 25(6), 462-496, https://www.emerald.com/insight/content/doi/10.1108/17542411011069882/f ull/html

Tolar, M. (2012). Mentoring experiences of high-achieving women. *Advancing in Developing Human Resources, 14(1)*, 172, https://journals.sagepub.com/doi/abs/10.1177/1523422312436415

Tomas, M., Lavie, J., Duran, M., & Guillamon, C. (2012). Women in academic administration at the university.

Educational Management Administration and Leadership, 38(1), 487-502, https://journals.sagepub.com/doi/abs/10.1177/1741143210368266

Torras, M., & Grow, J. (2015). Creative women in Peru: Outliers in a mschismo world. Communicacio'n y Sociedad; *Pamplona, 28(2),* 1-18, https://search.proquest.com/openview/aaa88b539fb79568debc33d8e0266604/1?p q-origsite=gscholar&cbl=18750&diss=y

Tsegay, T. (2013). Some Ethiopian women leaders' perception about their leadership. *Advancing Women in Leadership, 1(33),* 75-86, https://awl-ojs-tamu.tdl.org/awl/index.php/awl/article/view/97

Twombly, S. B. (1998). Women academic leaders in a Latin American university: Reconciling the paradoxes of professional lives. *Higher Education,* 35(4), 367– 397, https://link.springer.com/article/10.1023/A:1003165822754

U.S. Census Bureau (2012). *Women by the Numbers.* Retrieved June 9, 2020 from: https://www.census.gov/library/visualizations/2019/comm/women-at-work.html

U.S. Department of Commerce. (2012). *American fact finder table b17010: Poverty status in the past 12 months of families.* Retrieved June 9, 2020 from: https://www.census.gov/data/tables/time-series/demo/income-poverty/cps- pov/pov-01.html

U.S. Department of Education (2010). *The Condition of education.* Retrieved June 9, 2020 from:

https://nces.ed.gov/pubsearch/pubsinfo.asp?pubid=2010028

U.S. Department of Labor and the Bureau of Labor Statistics. (2011, January). *Workforce statistics for 2010.* http://www.bls.gov/iag/tgs/iag70.htm

Valentora, J., Otta, E., Silva, M., & McElligott, A. (2017*). Underrepresentation of women in the senior levels of brazilian science.* https://peerj.com/articles/4000.pdf

Vegard J, (2016) "Gender and self-employment: the role of mini-companies", *Education + Training,* 58(2),150-163, https://doi-org.contentproxy.phoenix.edu/10.1108/ET-06-2015-0051

Van Vianen, A. E. M., & Fischer, A. H. (2002). Illuminating the glass ceiling: The role of organizational culture preferences. *Journal of Occupational and Organizational Psychology,* 75(1), 315–338, https://onlinelibrary.wiley.com/doi/abs/10.1348/096317902320369730

Voepel, M. (2017). *Women in Athletic Departments: Welcomed or Marginalized.* https://www.espn.com/espnw/culture/feature/story/_/id/19686799/women-athletic-departments-welcomed-marginalized

Vinney, C. (2018). *Understanding social identity theory and its impact on behavior. thought co.* https://www.thoughtco.com/social-identity-theory-4174315

Vollmer, S., & Howard, G. (2010). Statistical power, the Belmont report, and the ethics of clinical trials. *Science and*

Engineering Ethics, 16 (4), 675-691, https://link.springer.com/article/10.1007/s11948-010-9244-0

Voss, K., & Speere, L. (2014). Taking chances and making changes: The career paths and pitfalls of pioneering women in newspaper management. *Journalism & Mass Communication Quarterly*, 91(1), 272-288, https://journals.sagepub.com/doi/abs/10.1177/1077699014527453

Ward, M. (2019). *Wage gap persists for women in north Carolina's finance industry.*

North Carolina Business News. https://www.bizjournals.com/charlotte/news/2019/01/02/wage-gap-persists-for-women-in-north-carolina-s.html

Webb, E.J., Campbell, D.T., Schwartz, R.D., & Sechrest, L. (1966). Unobtrusive measures: Nonreactive measures in the social sciences. Rand McNally.

Weyer, B. (2007). Twenty years later: Explaining the persistence of the glass ceiling for women leaders. *Women in Management Review, (22)6,* 482-496, https://www.emerald.com/insight/content/doi/10.1108/09649420710778718/full/html

White, K. (2003). Women and leadership in higher education in Australia. *Tertiary Education and Management, 9(1),* 45–60, https://www.tandfonline.com/doi/abs/10.1080/13583883.2003.9967092

Williams, S. (2013). *What is gender discrimination in the workplace?* http:// www.eHow.com

Wolfe, L. (2019). *Gender and sex discrimination in the Workplace*. Women in Business. https://www.thebalancecareers.com/gender-sex-discrimination-examples-3515723

Workplace Bullying (2008). *The WBI U.S. workplace bullying survey*. http:// www.workplacebullying.org

Wylie, K., dos Santos, P. (2016). A Law on paper only: Electoral rules, parties, and the persistent underrepresentation of women in Brazilian legislatures. *Politics & Gender; Cambridge 12(3)*, 415-442, https://www.academia.edu/download/54001440/WylieDosSantos_PAG16_FirstVi ew.pdf

Yin, R. (2014). *Case study research: design and methods: Fourth Edition.* SAGE Publications. Thousand Oaks, CA

Zenger, J. (2017). *3 Reasons To recruit and select more female leaders.* https://www.forbes.com/sites/jackzenger/2017/06/22/3-reasons-to-recruit-and- select-more-female-leaders/#7c66076530b4

Definition of Terms

Discrimination – was an action that denied social participation or human rights to categories of people that was based on prejudice (Cambridge Dictionary, 2013). That included treatment of an individual or group that was based on their actual or perceived membership in a certain group or social category, "in a way that was worse than the way people were usually treated (Cambridge Dictionary, 2013)."

Glass ceiling theory- was an invisible barrier that prevented women from being promoted to executive level positions even if they were qualified to do so (FGCC, 1995).

The Glass cliff theory- suggested that when women did come into leadership positions, it was usually an organization that was going through a crisis and where also the risk of failure is higher (Smith, 2015).

Leadership – was a process whereby an individual influenced a group of individuals to achieve a common goal (Northouse, 2012).

Role congruity theory – considered the gender role of the individual, the congruity with other roles, and behavior that was prejudicially associated with the role (Eagly & Karau, 2002).

Senior-leadership positions- Those positions included CEOs, Executives, and Upper Management (Smith, 2015).

Sex-role stereotypes theory – occurred when individuals were expected to enact certain practices or behaviors because of their gender (Scantlebury, 2009).

About the Author

Dr. LaShanda N. Shaw has a passion for seeing women equally represented in the workplace.

As a young child, Dr. Shaw set her sights on becoming a leader in her career field of choice. Her experiences in various leadership roles, gave awareness to the lack of equality in the workplace for women in senior level positions.

She dedicates her time to help woman within the community through her foundation *The Pedestal*, which is about building women's self-esteem as leaders and in their own personal lives. Dr. Shaw endeavors to equip and empower the future leaders with tools, resources and skills to navigate the road to success.

Born and raised in Fayetteville, NC, Dr. Shaw holds a Bachelor of Science Degree in Entrepreneurship, a Master's in Business Administration and a Doctorate of Management in Organizational Leadership. She is the Broker-in-Charge of LaShanda Shaw Realty and Owner and Creative Director of *BLEED FOR FASHION*.

The importance of faith, the respect for family and

love for fashion keeps her well-rounded and focused as she advocates on behalf of women in leadership and those seeking leadership positions. Dr. LaShanda Shaw knows that everyone is not a leader, whether a man or a woman, but believes that opportunities for such leadership positions should be available and fairly obtained by all.

Connect with the Author

LaShanda.shaw@yahoo.com

www.lashandashaw.wixsite.com/drlashandashaw

Made in the USA
Middletown, DE
16 November 2023

42672971R00071